CW01281610

Homily

Homily

being
*chants for Christians, Socialists, all of isms,
or those finding faith, not seeking belief,
in the layout of my 19 Liners*
being
poems of spirituality for maybe some soulfulness

Snowdon Barnett

Rivelin Grapheme Press

First published in 2014 by Rivelin Grapheme Press,
The Pavilion, Kintbury, Berkshire, RG17 9TU,
in a limited edition of 500 copies of which 26 are lettered A to Z and each
are signed by Poet and Illustrator.

10 9 8 7 6 5 4 3 2 1

© Snowdon Barnett 2014 whose right to be identified as the author of this work has been asserted in accordance with the Copyright Designs and Patents Act 1988.

All rights reserved. No part of this publication may be reproduced, stored in a retrieval system or transmitted in any form or by any means, electronic, mechanical, photocopying, recording, digital or otherwise, without the prior written permission of the author.

A CIP catalogue record for this book is available from the British Library.

ISBN 094761243-2
978094612436

Printed and bound in England by The Lavenham Press.

Contents

Note on the Illustrations		x
Preface		xi
Unit One:	Kyrie	1

Four Mystic Alones		3
	sola Scriptura	4
	sola gratia	5
	solo Christo	6
	sola fide	7

Some Songs

Introduction into Four Servant Songs		8
First	*Servant as Prophet*	9
Second	*Servant as Missionary*	10
Third	*Servant as Sage*	11
Fourth	*Servant as Forerunner*	12
Song of Miriam		13
Song of Deborah		14
Song of Sophia		15

Hymns & Prayers

Hymn One:	Philippians 2: vv 6-11	16
Two:	Colossians 1: vv 15-20	17
Three:	1 Timothy 3: vv 14-16	18
Four:	1 Corinthians 16 v22	19

Nature of Use of Prayer
    One: *of prayer between persons*   20
    Two: *of some divine*   21
    Three: *of answers*   22
    continuous prayer   23
    meditation upon *Job's Poem*   24

Introduction into St Paul's Journeys into Significance   25
    First Journey   26
    Other Journeyings   27
    Last Journey   28
with Pauline Remembrancer   29

Unit Two: Gloria   31

    ad fontes   32
    advice for a young poet   33
    Myths in Northern Mists   34
    towards a new poetics (reprise)   35
    as to wastefulness in any language   36
    this little light of mine   37
    into vague language   38
    an attempted *Spiritual Aeneid*   39
    Neither Minor Nor Neglect   40
    Tonight   41

Unit Three:	Credo	43
	in this cleft stick	44
	Abandonment	45
	John's *problematic texts*	46
	Canticle of Canticles	47
	as to problematic texts	48
	reflecting Apocryphal Gospels	49
	de-attribution	50
	a Book of Hours	51
	too many souls	52
	from *Calvary* to *Bethany*	53
	an Easter affirmation	54
	Jesus as hamper for life	55
Unit Four:	Sanctus	57
	absence of Karma in Capricorn	58
	imaginal	59
	Purusha	60
	Refreshments from Rumi	61
	His *incarnational presence*	62
	veriditas	63
	theism?	64
	Dweller on the Threshold	65
	in partibus infedelium	66
	only is *God* is only	67

Unit Five:	Benedictus	69
	espadrilles	70
	Towards those *Domes of Omdurman*	71
	wishin' nor' nor' west	72
	Seventh Seal	73
	Viaticum	74
	Isms (rarely are)	75
	ficciones	76
	where is the fate of *orality*	77
	perhaps some ultimate meaninglessness of *things*	78
	vain repetition	79
	Inchabod	80
	dust & ashes	81
	This Much I Know	82
	Word	83
Unit Six:	Agnus Dei	85
Ten Poems	*as to the way we live now*	86

triptych on economics

	austerity in encumbered times	87
	an end with money	88
	easy cash remaining instantaneous corrupter	89

triptych *on politics*

	as to on-street parking	90
	as to confusions of coalition	91
	as to porism	92

triptych *on society*

	deliver not de-lever	93
	attempting orderly disposals of disorderly libraries	94
	having by-passed another ungrateful day	95

resumé (is 1875's craft still girt?)	96
Fifteen Poems a*s three Quintets*	97

First Quintet :   as to *infrequency of meetings*

armistice	98
re-union	99
this *thing* itself	100
some *via media*	101
of *everlastingness*	102

Second Quintet :   as to *five centuries of protest*

of *this spiritual principle*	103
this *spiritual presence*	104
ultramontane	105
of *spiritual wisdom*	106
towards five hundred	107

Third Quintet :   as to *an ending*

gratia infusa	108
ras el hanout	109
humour me	110
after *charisma*	111
in concluding : *on colour*	112
Addendum	113
Afterword	115
The Author's published poetry	123

Note on the Illustrations

The illustrations merit a special mention. When my elder brother, Winston, saw an early draft of some of these poems, he was inspired by T.S. Eliot's *The Hollow Men*[1] to prepare a series of fifteen Images and until quite recently they were all arranged to appear in this Collection.

At that time my Illustrator commented:
> *The imagery evoked by Eliot's poem is complex in his redrawing landscapes and his re-imagining of the human figure is a recurring and constant feature. It is axiomatic that whilst the image of a human figure, individually or in groups, can be arresting and compelling, those cannot compete with the uniqueness, and depth, of the image when reduced to the scale of a portrait.*
> *So here the images selected that relate or pay homage to Eliot's text, are imagined portraits, not full length figures, and are each set in a specific context drawn from quoted lines in the poem. Focusing on the head alone, and not on an overall image of the figure, aids and supports that concentration and rumination which text deserves if not demands.*

However, when I restructured the work into the present six sections, I asked him to draw Decorated Initials and it became apparent to us both that his Images overreached those Initials. Therefore, now only two are placed in the Addendum with another pair comprising the front and rear covers.

I hope his Images would encourage a reader to purchase Eliot's work. I did request consent from Faber and Faber but heard nothing.

---

1 1925, from *Selected Poems*, Faber and Faber, 1954, but as republished in their 80th Anniversary Collection of 2009.

Preface

This word *homily* has been defined as
> *especially a practical discourse with a view to the spiritual edification of the hearers, rather than for the development of a doctrine or theme*[1].

My *Homily* is part of a natural progression from the spiritual poems in *Once in a Blue Moon*, through *Nocturne* and into *Feasts of Devotion*.

I am moved by the fact that 31st October 2017 will be the five-hundredth anniversary of whatever Martin Luther did on that day in 1517 and I present this group of poems as my own personal remembrancer of that. I am not so much concerned as to how the *Reformation* occurred or the interpretation of the *Eucharist*, neither as to how *Mass* or *Communion* or *The Lord's Supper* be performed, nor whatever legacy has been left behind and rests uneasily amongst believers of whichever *faith* today, but more as to it being, perhaps   *too much of head*
too little of heart
that has caused me to consider after some five hundred years the state and condition of spirituality in this society which seems to me to be at one and the same time to be endeavouring to focus information which is accessible world-wide upon some insular and particularly parochial. In doing so I extend beyond the *Holy Scriptures* into many other revered texts, endeavouring to capture that which evolves through some devotional into mystical.

My introduction to this collection of 95 new poems is the quartet which comprises *Four Mystic Alones*. Those four poems are focused on that which I believe may remain of *Reformation* and are written as beacons to guide.

---

1 Oxford English Dictionary, Clarendon Press, Oxford, 1933, Vol V. (H-K).

for
Winston

*if I can't bide with you on the Bridge
let's abide forever by the Riverside*

KYRIE

Four Mystic Alones

sola Scriptura	with *Word* alone
sola gratia	by grace alone
solo Christo	in *Christ* alone
sola fide	through faith alone

These are reminders of that which remains from Martin Luther's protest being his *Disputation for the purpose of explaining the efficacy of the Indulgence*; his ninety-five propositions. Tradition has it that he posted these on the door of the Castle Church at Wittenburg on 31st October 1517. My four *alones* constitute remaining cornerstones of *Reformation*. Verbs may direct steps towards belief, but it is fundamental nouns which declare unshakeable faith.

In this, my personal eulogy for John Nelson Darby, I acknowledge *Sola Scriptura*, published by the Reformation Trust, Ligonier Ministries, Orlando, Florida, Second Edition, 2009.

It is not without interest that this collection contains *Ninety-five Poems*.

sola Scriptura

with *Word* alone

it is a good & acceptable perfection that all will be transformed
conforming through metamorphis to an incarnate
of mind's wisdom, all foolishness discard
in moving through these passages to inspiration
avoid noise & its background of confusion

whilst others compose *book-based* ever only second-hand impressions,
here as to revelation each page turns to truth
as unity appears often as camouflage to compromise
love inhabits truth as often as truth inhibits love

is knowledge to be frozen into time's hands' illuminated manuscripts

it is essential to remain that correct person
surrounded by uncorrupted texts
fore-wondering what those words are for

only this can nullify that wedge between science & scripture
only through your own practice can this *Word* spring to life
only by constant recitation may doubt be expunged

in this light from your own lamp let these words speak bright

concentrate upon experiential peace of poetry

text apply to yourself and you to your own text

sola gratia

by grace alone

I must be prudent and not protest too much
I need be catholic in both opinion and taste
I aim to paint my catechism into rainbows of promise

to satisfy my soul's insatiable appetite
to transcend my own self-consciousness
to achieve a decorum of decent devotion

I must remain constant in thought, undistracted
by structures interfering with spaces between
that place which only grace alone may occupy

from this meaninglessness of mere existence

if I am to be enabled to carry cups to those others enfeebled
if I am to experience descent from some seventh heaven
if I am to become my own & contemplative quietist

I can concentrate upon my daydreams
I may escape this nightmare of day-being
of worry, of food, of money, of possessions, of debts,
of dreaming, of succeeding into some lottery of troves,

I'm straining so hard into not doing what I must not do
I'm finding it harder to strive to doing what I ought to do

solo Christo

in *Christ* alone

laws written in blood, bleed away
as lunacy in one generation is sanity to another

book writings in religious tomes
fall as pressed leaves, petals of hopelessness

as oral traditions are traduced to print
no matter their degree of obscurity
all may be infallibly discerned
for some long-awaited Teacher from some New World
breathing natural, perhaps spiritual, laws

ex nihilo, nihil fit

as I surrender myself into his dissonance of colour
that *is-ness* Eckehart saw and Hopkkins held as *thing*
I am reflecting inside, this, my own I

speaking of lands between shores of births, of deaths
is all of life gentle regret or merely mild amusement
some eucalyptus leaf refusing its decay

lands where ghosts have lost all consequence
where each winds up in wraiths

All remains in All if each resides in All

sola fide

through faith alone

I have trodden this wine-press alone
(on a pilgrim's path not all is as wise as is perceived)

over everything has been drawn blankets of doubts
a confusion of thinking aloud, speakers or preachers
a preponderance of questioning
instead of heeding answers nature screams to us
in folds of hillsides, in singing of flowing waters
by those lights twinkling between clouds
into distancing of sacred traditions

ours may become (maybe has always been) truly ours

I may rest beneath Heaven's dome of lapis-lazuli
no hynagogic visionary necessary for me
that sublime holiness to which man aspires
everything remaining intrinsically insignificant
into that *allness* which is an infinity of *being*

may I perceive just one colour in a corner of Eden's garden
whilst my undernourished ego diminishes me
ignoring tones, receiving only varieties in shades

sola gratia, solo Christo, sola fide

Introduction into Four Servant Songs

These four *Servant Songs* point towards *Resurrection*. They envisage and herald that new beginning when those dead on earth shall be re-born into heavenly bodies. This is the complete mystery of this *New Covenant* which is foretold in various segments of the *Old*, such as these, which since being classified by Duhm in his *Commentary* of 1892, have spawned much more to which I only add these four all arising from the *Book of Isaiah* as to:

	First	*42 vv 1 to 4*
	Second	*49 vv 1 to 6*
	Third	*50 vv 4 to 9*
	Fourth	*52 v 13 to 53 v 12*

(this numbering being my own choice).

An obvious difficulty in constructing four such poems of equal length is that those first three sets of verses total together only 16 whereas the fourth has 58, which makes me conclude that they should be considered as one wholeness. However, because chapter 53 is so well trod, I have chosen to side-step the more familiar of its verses.

In these poems, it is this lord speaking of and to his servant, of whom all may be. I take my central and link line *coasts & islands* from *The New Jerusalem Bible*, Darton, Longman & Todd, London 1985 and I acknowledge them for that.

First Song of the Servant

Servant as Prophet

here is my servant he is here
delighting my soul my chosen own
my spirit as dove resting upon his dome

waiting for his laws, for his earthly judgments
to bring forth truth, no smoking flax

his voice is stilled by night-time's longerings
those lingering in streets below heed nothings
as he turns away from breaking his crushed reed
from snuffing-out all flickering wickednesses from

coasts & islands

I have excited him to prophecy
for which he must desert his own desert
to bring fair dealings to everyone everywhere

through him will I reveal all futures
I who created you and all other *things*
to those blind incarcerate I will enlighten sight

no one may crush my servant in his mission
through his words I breathe out my own spirit
faithfully he presents my present of resurrection

Second Song of the Servant

Servant as Missionary

all those inhabiting separate archipelagoes
listen to my servant
his tongue is my sharp sword
my arrow in this quiver of my womb

my servant hides hidden in the shadow of my hand
I present through him my light of salvation
which will persevere to his indemnity

in his travels and travails there will be sufferings
but doom shall not prevail as his *Word* is my word throughout

coasts & islands

my Songs are Parables
my Songs foretell my Resurrection
my Songs are manifestations of my Glories

I have pronounced his name to my memory
I am his strength & his honour reflects in my eye
his cause is mine which speaks his recompense

is he to exhaust himself to no purpose
is his epitaph to be

my toiling has been mere futility

Third Song of the Servant

Servant as Sage

in courts of this morning of your resurrection
hear my servant present his argument

learnéd tongues make me unashamed
as sheep at shearing bleat some discontent

each morning my voice whispers an ear
of comfort to his weariness
an ear nor turned away nor spurned
listening as disciples listen
with their tongues stilled across

coasts & islands

my servant has suffered for his sagacity
it is myself they insult who spit and strike at him
& in my service he turns his face away

this is my servant's perfection in obedience
as all others wax old as garments moths devour

& as my books are opened & as my saints are named
those who have scorned that *Easter Moment,* my servant
will cast aside into an eternity of tombstones & of graves

my servant's face is set as a flint is sealed

Fourth Song of the Servant

Servant as Forerunner

I close my eyes, my ears
as death in vain my *Word* would swallow up
but silence in full face of sorrows always vindicates
& through knowledge of my servant all souls' travails shall pass away

as a sapling my servant shall prosper
rising as an Ark on Ararat
as my servant's good pleasure's to crush
out all of life from those
living in wickedness and rebellion's delusions on their

coasts & islands

from this Song many more may chorus
from his sufferings all will bleed redemption
from this sacrifice shall spring everlasting love & peace

this is my foretaste of each & every Easter Sunday morning
as I tend as shepherd to my servant lamb who strays

my servant sought no reward but mine is his
as from all that was foretold has been revealed
& now he rests forever by my right side &

here is my servant he is here

Song of Miriam

*her song is of faith in her lord because
if we have such, he will surge and each and
every rider and their chariot will be thrown into sea's thrash*

& so Miriam
with her timbrel to her hand-maid
her women after her
singing & dancing
for their contrivances

& she mouthed him Moses
having drawn him out from waters
breached for his birth
& she had nursed him for Pharaoh's daughter

& now she joins into his chantings of anthems

where nothing may divide nor spoil
where lust shall not be satiate
where swords shall stay safe-sheaved

as their lordship glorious in holiness appears
as those fearful reach wonders through praises
as Miriam's faithful nestle by her sanctuary of bulrushes

red-drowned horses & riders by their reed-full sea
with murmurings stilled
& so bitter waters at Marah flow betimes & so

Song of Deborah

diatribe against destruction

her palm beneath, Deborah her
prophetess & priestess, wife & judgment-mother
entitled to her rest, her heavenly peace

contained within histories are narratives into truth
circulating uncertain questions as to time & tense

is there some meaning in these meanderings of clouds
wisdom's lost across breaths of saints

I've glanced that sharpness in her nail, her hammer hand
his stricken head, his temple overthrown, destroyed

those servants of their lord do not commiserate

now glorious with her past with all intents outside
her heart has trembled as her heavenly waters flow,
she sings her song, her needlework of diverse hues
has stilled his chariot's wheels as lattice-work despoiled

her song prevails as prelude to her peacefulness
women-folk would ever seek emasculate their kind
battlefields of wars are blood-stained by the brute force of men

had he requested rest, would he have been allowed to sleep

her lands subsuming into peace for forty years

Song of Sophia

song to redemption

today & everyday are now my dancing days
my reaching to ineffable light
through mysteries, through higher space
as this light-wreath rests upon my brow
ascending me to heights of eagle's lightness
saving me from chaos left below

this earthly ministry, my Master's force turns supra-cosmic
separating spiritual souls from bodies politic
unmixing orthodoxy from simplicities of faith

singing to legends of logos

& as my soul disgorge my body
my afterlife, sublime, mysterious & wonderful
entering palaces to be re-united with sleeping shapes
angelic forms possess my individuality
through esoteric symbolism
where absence of wealth accentuates worth

there in that ineffable & divine light of peace
welcomed into their Midst to comprehend all Mysteries
may become humble helper in his Treasury of doing

Hymn One
Philippians 2: vv 6-11

who being holy formed
grasped no equality from form
but emptied into humanity
humbled an acceptance towards death
gifting as Lord as Kyrios his resurrection
into my own self unholy & unformed

where is he who breathes my breath away
why am I so uncertain in his simplistic presence
how may I become emptied into his equality

hum your own hymnal towards christological heights

here may I address what qualifies as *hymn*
ignoring that vexéd question *what be poetry*
which appears to exist outside of time but within form

I seize outwith these verses his generosity of soul
turning my poverty into riches of his spirit
there is no greater prize than puzzling over love

I have metamorphosized formality into formalism
I wheel in my barrow all these theophanies
I hear such cries of woe from *Valleys of Hymnology*

Hymn Two
Colossians 1 :vv 15-20

first-borne & beginner
supreme within creative presence
reconciler of this whole universe
overseer of her return to peaceful order
principal in this new promise of salvation
making visible to all your own invisible

in hypothesis resides reality's problems
never question futility in any quest
redact each day remembrance of yesterday

this is my own my chrisological hymnal

here I am in tune with Wisdom's singing
as all *things* may describe towards celestial
angels and humans forever reconciled

imagining this image of souls invisible
first born, re-born, now ever-born
into revelation's re-creation throughout eternity

each beginning is only a preliminary struggle with mortality
as he beguiles with persuasive power
besets an indwelling profundity of this cosmic *christos*

Hymn Three
1 Timothy 3:vv 14-16

made visible into flesh
justified through angelic spirits
proclaimed, translated, glorified

from this pastoral epistle
observe mysteries throughout pieties
each answer encrypted as chiastic
heaven & earth forming no contest save contrast
all as unified into universal personality
each stone, belief, supporting its roof of faith

within christological hymns some new-ness celebrate within

only by reflecting upon fragments of broken promises
only by collecting up shards of unfulfilled desirings
can currencies of mercies circulate
can forgiveness of errors forge further misunderstandings

consider across absences of separateness
how ineffective undelivered missives may appear to be

my faith appears founded upon ancestral traditions
yet it requires its daily shot of cantharides

try tabling a farewell discourse to a dry old corpse

Hymn Four
I Corrinthians 16 v 22
& so cry *Maran atha*

death in babtism harbours no dangers for death
shredding trappings of mortalities
this physical only points to parasceve
this nowness of resurrection
this fullness to redemption

in this second coming of my lord
are all my hopes fulfilled
though difficulties abide
within renditions of these texts

Lord acknowledge him as Nazareth Man

lord acknowledge us his fellow men
another as disciple acknowledge one another
all arise together acknowledging his lordship's all

unpredictability in this my journey
resolves me that my destination has not passed
yet is here and is to appear yet

I seek neither life after death
nor some part of existence apart from death
but my lord's eternal experience through immortal death

Prayer: *its nature & use*

Poem One : *of prayer between persons*

exaggerate all vocatives & blend each voice to pray
surrender up each sophism of soul of sense

continuous praying is an osmosis of persuasion
silent whist *He* breathes out *His* silence
my words inadequate affront his *Word's* true eloquence
prayer reflects as mirror, soul's own existence

seeking to remove Isis' veil
presuming my conscience in my Master's voice
permitting some higher to entreat my lower plea

prayer precipitates its own prayer

remaining as rhetoric but never logical
that insidiousness inside which motivates outside
providing whatever may be divinely prescribed
dousing off eternal bleakness into clouds of knowing

my person is not one only but one of too many
where abides no unity in this my own self-centredness

Sunday religions beget comforts to bodies, all & sundry,
so am I enabled to escape my womb of doubt

apologia pro vita sua

Prayer: *its nature & use*

Poem Two : *of some divine*

prayer illuminates whoever prays within a light of love
mystical self-abandonment refills absences
souls as specks off that almighty soul

there needs an invocation between minds at prayer
beseeching divineness as inner silentness
passivity does not denote inertia
mystical life need not be solitary darkness
spiritual activity must always produce practical results
an openness to all realities

this world's not hostile, hostility's in man

meditating upon my Mediator through his own prayer
not by magical incantation, of song, of dance,
but through abandoning illusion, adopting wisdom

neither is it chatter or gossip or reportage
not theatre nor is it enigmatic utterance

purpose of prayer is for provision for faith
for matters malleable for minds

eliminate each vocative, leaving as my prayer

in nominee Jesu

Prayer: *its nature & use*

Poem Three : *of answers*

divine nature may appear incomprehensible
opening closed doors into windows of knowledge, of truth

absorbing this paradox of transcendent reality
do not request a cross, only help bear those of others
discard rags of poverty, don garments of pure gold
pray for an impossible & possibilities may appear
as there is so little probable for me to see as

in any room full of believers there is loneliness & solitude
each moving inside each one's own inconostasis

pray that I am as some curve, unconscious of my asymptotic prayer

christians from his crib and to his cross
all shuffle backwards into an unreality of sense
this whole of science as of art may be their prayer
all individualities collectively presented, all correct

ignore those intrigues into sacristies
deficiencies in the partiality of parochial records
step back to analyse this mass of prayer
these answers heard in silence not presumed

vigilate et orate

continuous prayer

averse not reciting verse
move a body's strength to her other side
allow insides meld to listeners' outside
step forward & blend to truth with light

Jesus was particular with prayer
simply requesting all of prayer to Jesu

everything in *Me* not *Me* in everything
so never lost
to me he's never lost to me

in this garden of prayers' uninterrupted peacefulness

his Saints are not created naked not to dress
address his holy face reflected through his grace
his image is as polish on a burnished chalice
admire in holiness his spiritual presence
his followers measuring equality unto righteousness

lawful prayers are merely contradictions against wilfullness
seeking interfacing connections

god's prayer continuing through my prayer to gods

I used to care but now care not I

meditation upon *Job's Poem*
ex re nata

whoever you were – wherever you are
from antiquities of sufferings into sorrows
availing Wisdom's children of their East
as captivity approaches slowly closing gates
changing alphabets into psalms or proverbs

reflecting rewards of righteousness through their prosperity
whilst those in their goodly service overcome their rejected
earing to his lord's twin voices erring
eyeing not with blind intellect but with faith's own eye

presumption preferred above church orthodoxy

those agéd mouth their theology but not by inspiration
only by rote as road signs warn off soft-verges
seeking to look when only feeling's possible
across these great divides of oceans and of seas

this power in expiation conceals each mystery in creation
rather than troubling mindlessness, search endlessly through truth's
embarrassments of fellow-traveller's false doctrines
be sublime, contrite, as unridiculous as is right

erubescent in my own & quietly decomposing sense of ersatz

Introduction into St Paul's Journeys into Significance

These evolved following my re-visiting H.V. Morton's *In the Steps of St Paul* (Rich & Cowan, London 1936) where he recounts his own rather than this Apostle's steps and so these are my own and, as such, are only tentative.

In these poems I have approximated his words as I write below a blue sky of faith while acknowledging dangerous depths of waters beneath.

I do not believe that these journeys were to establish new communities of believers. Arithmetically, Paul can only be associated with seven such. During his testimony many others must have seeded into bloom.

While travelling, he is firing off encyclical (sometimes intemperate) letters in a self-same six-fold structure as:

>*salutation*
>*thanksgiving*
>*prayer for well-being*
>*accounting of practical holiness*
>*with encouragement*
>*followed by his own somewhat pious conclusion*

As in *Four Servant Songs* I begin with that lord's voice but in these pieces that of St Paul encroaches as, indeed, it must.

First Journey

Antioch to Asia Minor (with Barnabas)

it is not simple scribbling to those strangers
straggling along behind their individual bands of hope
(perhaps I voiced myself too angrily to those within Galatia)

is there any purpose to all of this travelling
which seemingly adds nothing to my journeying

I tread upon unmade tracks to form this my new way
to hope to watch my fruits of faith
silently presenting themselves in unkempt hedgerows
an ephemeris rarely yields fruition's promise

turning geographical into theological byeways

if I could foresee those trials, these tribulations
warings & widowings & angst & angers
would I pen another word or prefer to peevishness in penury
to laze upon this languid harbour's home

but a missionary's work is not to question buts
but to present in evidence what buts no buts
to disregard all buts to dis-belief
to butter up upon his way through ghee to glee

my servant now with faith re-fires my light

Other Journeyings (*embracing Two and Three*)

around Aegean Sea with Silas & involving Timothy

from my view here revealed into Macedonia
this good news
to Lydia in purple purpose to her livelihood

& now earthquakes awakening
saving some gaolor saving his household
& further entrities & nearer alarums
under covers of darkness these servants escape
my journeys' catalogue catastrophe
burning souls imprint into life's burning

moving place to place, soul to soul, face to face

I touch all heartlands, beating souls in love
releasing heaving passions from loving hearts eternal

I've asked myself what purpose to their journeyings
or whatever will determine life as failure
perhaps all livelihoods begin with Moses in his basket

to visit each & every city's centre-place
to preach, to invigorate, to sanctify
to bless each stone, to contain each life its own

spirit's force in baptism regenerating each soul to power

Last Journey

from Caesarea (maybe involuntarily)

let ignorance roam especially within Rome

inside my silent sorrow after my full week of work
at tents & other apparatus for just journeyings
my letters from my ports of call to other's callings
are as my roll-call to those saved, those blesséd

I go wherever his message suffers me
to turn this world completely upside down

I am ready not only to be bound but bound to die am I
ever obedient to my heavenly vision's ever

as minister & as witness

as in my endless voyagings I'd dreamt of drifting upon rocks
facing arrest & sailing out of Caesarea facing death
releasing to this world my writings into faith
essentially confident in my lord's work

my fourth and final journey from which I do not now recoil
involving (as it does) involuntary sailors' shipwrecks
which I accept to be within my lordship's vision
but I am blinded by his tremors of truth's lightenings

this work to his redemption remains as incomplete

Pauline Remembrancer
lex orandi, lex credenti

following (hard upon heels) those four Evangelists
replacing them as corner-stones
ensuring heaven's Byzantium dome belies collapse

I stirred myself at first in halls of ignorance
crowded with cultural clutter of class
when whorls from skies would energize
& I saw in clouds my own, my lotus jewel
transforming to performing his redemptive powers
binding all on earth as all unbinds in heaven

there's more effort in forgetting than in remembering

as I sail uncertain of my future
parting insecurely with my past
I am cast out as anchor
fearing least chains are sheared to become outcast

remembrancing is effort's vainness never to forget
it's too easy to become, *en route* of doubts, shipwrecked
doubting what may be purposeful throughout travelling escapades

am I as unsure of my future, insecure in my departed past, as I am

is revision wrong or is reform just a new is

GLORIA

ad fontes
avoiding *Antinomianism*

law derides if rules are divisive & regulations confusing
is justification by faith alone its own licence *à la* 007
laws devoid of fear of punishment are merely laxitives

is anyone under law for judgment only & not for good conduct
does anybody not reconstruct some own self-righteousness
maybe only this gospel sweetens bitterness which laws impose

bring to this table souls of strength, hearts binding minds,
closing into your lord in prayer but never closing
sourcing all in love not fear

those works to supererogation

I'm commanded, may vice be forbidden
I'm forbidden, may duty be commended

these are everywhere irregulars of omission or commission

evidence is ever rumour disputed through other's evidence
evidence is alas only manipulated into other evidence

pursuing spirit over flesh, choose to be singular,
law's purpose is to promote freedom into liberty
where, in an ending to endeavour, revives *Holy Spirit's* power

& all into each one's source of love not fear

advice for a young poet
after *Rainer Maria Rilke*

philosophers may fail but will poets prevail
each word in each poem must be keystone
poetry is not built on cornerstones of mausoleums

there's nothing such as her *one moment in time*
time is only some special entity within eternity
moments are of no earthly matter

no one may advise yourself as you've no-one to
loosen your shift to ponder upon your breast
only by entering inside yourself can you become as one *only*

compose and grave each letter as Rainer could

in this hopelessness which is this riddle of life's
contingencies, try to avoid personal contagions

there is something sickly in someone's discarded under-clothing
where feminine will always relish whatever is unfruitful

tending towards understatement is as nothing towards tenderness
perfection in birth's bloods too swiftly bleeds away

embrace love & all emotions
eschew syntax & symbolism

be, just be, and in your own special being, be

Myths in Northern Mists
for *Basil Bunting*

returning to my Tyne my heart dished out
from liveries of cities loosed or lost
new watersfresh flow below this low swung bridge
trout salmon replenishing soils and sewers
I seek my own self by this new Millennium span

there are so many dead so far departed
so many pages written out of sense
so many bitter breaths of rant of roke
there are so many hearts past rousing

her photogenic glance has snapped my soul

turning now my time-spent dimmed down Northern lights
I've pleasing to my face soft Southern breezes
with lengthening into ease I'm leaving only
nulled anecdotes, no annotated diaries

maybe all that's needful's already shared or spent
now are only memories each from each other sent
maybe it was only ever this one breathe of candle's light
now burn off old lumber, take stock to start anew
harbour pure thoughts, abandon history's vapour

towards a new poetics (reprise)

poetry in Englishness has lost her way
too many formal gardens within box hedges

poets (as has been praised) should all be pantheists
preferring soul to self
not material not personal not egotistical
preferring spirituality to sufficiency
but finding *unto this end* fulfillment
& profundity into peacefulness of mindlessness
unstressed, unburdened, unallayed

not meekly seek but boldly seize each arbour's sacred sense

poetry needs a gardener's niche
where each & every delicate can propitiate
attentive borders, mixed herbaceous & procumbent lawns
not penned into some artificial symmetry
but as landscapes which may overrun horizons

poets need their own pretence, their pruning forks
in silence through their seasons stay their need to talk

avoiding, outwith religiosity, almost all of insincerity
enjoying in this occidental orangery their own and oriental *bhakti*

as to wastefulness in any language

gossip is as ignorance sprouting off intolerance
maelstrom off kitchen table blendness
(withdrawing force from evil ensures peacefulness endures)

wars recur upon their resultant poverties
enemies must be seen to endure as enemas
this present peace helpless against unseen presentations
striking each house-hold mortgage unendowed
cancelling out each high-street shopping farce
as politicians pretend to actualise new-found pretentiousness

peace produces her own anomalies

gossip (on this other hand) needs to Press to survive
requires unthinking minds to mouth out loud
(on an astral plane its irrelevance is plain)

force withdrawn removes and suppresses force
opens up divine eyes to our own open-ness

must we remain in this vacuum of quantitative easing
pushed up into some folly of décolletage

if you do not attend into your own gardens of verse
there will be no cure against weeds of verbiage

this little light of mine

they rarely speak to me those tomes from
silent shelves unless my fingers electrify their
shades uncovering scattering worms from
their slumbering in peaceful yearnings to no learnings

a library is a past-place unaneled
a priest's hole undisturbed
where thoughts are clouded into doubts
where pages may escape a regency of rules
there must always stand some stopped clock

time only measured into dust

I need to let them go their own waywardness
I have catalogued them all their chosen names
I have boxed them into corners of disorder
I need to escape self-centred tyrannies of bookishness

But I will not; truculent will I remain
as Casaubon frustrated his Elizabethan
methods & manners as fancies & fallacies

sparkled up his chimney once a fire of change has sparked

mice may scuffle whilst peacocks preen

into *vague language*
or *what is love*

only as one loves oneself
may embalming others out-breast true love's
embrace, heaving to hoping to earnestness of trueishness
alive in some perfection of harmony to unison

intensity forget, all fades to unconsciousness

individuals seeking their glue to non-individuality
saying *yes* meaning *no* or meaning *no* mouthing *yes*
& so no-one really may love anyone save themselves

love is unity in life & through its life there's love

truth conceiving into love mere consequence of truth

communion does not envisage contact
love of one only barely embracing love
love may not lust in an unholy communion of love's
perfect essence, its spices & its perfumes,
it's ever always, never altered, permanence,
its purity in hidden depths not in religious rites

whilst undressing, undo your ego, whilst
your gaze rests upon your body beautiful, your
holistic grail, your temple into holiness reposed as holy grail

an attempted *Spiritual Aeneid*
in our reach at last, Italy's ever-receding shore
vi.61

maybe I have not changed
but only this World changes in its *maybe's*

am I as one with Knox as pathetic ne'er drastic
how may I escape just one tenet of these tentacles
when this unholy spider's web is so whole-spun

after such lengthy engagement, this briefest honeymoon
or is it just growing up after groanings of adolescence
avoiding now all of violence for any conscribed by conscience
now beginning this only & forever just another *Prologue*

or let me lie here with my own farewells to those dead souls

maybe this Church may not be receptive of my own *maybe*
faith being his gift, not revealed theology
neither conflagration nor accidental conflation
but securing safe harbourage, disintegration of danger

should juvenilia be restricted or revisited
any writer's reaction on coming against an educated reader

one rich in wisdom attracts envy from those poor of spirit
as this *Book of Christianities* continues
wherein each dislimns all of ultramundane

Neither Minor Nor Neglect

To be some voice, minor or neglect
never is that worst of states
it gives all time as may be requisite to contemplate

If seven prizes were to hand
I could be number eight from an eighty thousand band
spurning their garlands having failed
to post my poem with their entry form in vain

a Poet only should be renownéd
when she (or he) is tone cold dead

as bye some time minorities neglect their poets' majority

I attend Readings of those Famous
in total anonymity
Harken to their stultified applause
but bear no enmity

And when I'm passed into some other's empathy
with noisy poets' loosely chattering teeth
then will I feel that silent echo into destiny
And feet (while leaving) de-mystify my feats

And on true whims of tastelessness may these my poems be traduced

Tonight
for *Matthew Arnold*

it's calm *tonight* that Doctor's sea
his watchfulness on *Dover Beach* rests further east
but here by Bournemouth's *sandbanks*, blackness mystifies
tonight my search for faith tides out of truth

behind me there's too much twinkling to modernity
of lights of sounds slight heard as waves give way
& break upon these narrow shores brief marks of tides
detritus shuffling out my candle's flame to prayer
with souls of men, spirits of saints, angels of delightfulness

it needs not be so dark as this

am I watching a washing away of England's protestors
through remorseless intensity of waters breaking onto slivers
chasing lost moralities of charities through *drink ′n′ drugs*
it's so much easier to reach for stars than realise mind's psalms

my lord shall always still these waterways for faithful crafts
faith found refills unfaithfulness through memories
quicksilver glancing golden grains of shimmering sands
draws through believers' nets silvery flickering fish

it needs not always be so dark as this

CREDO

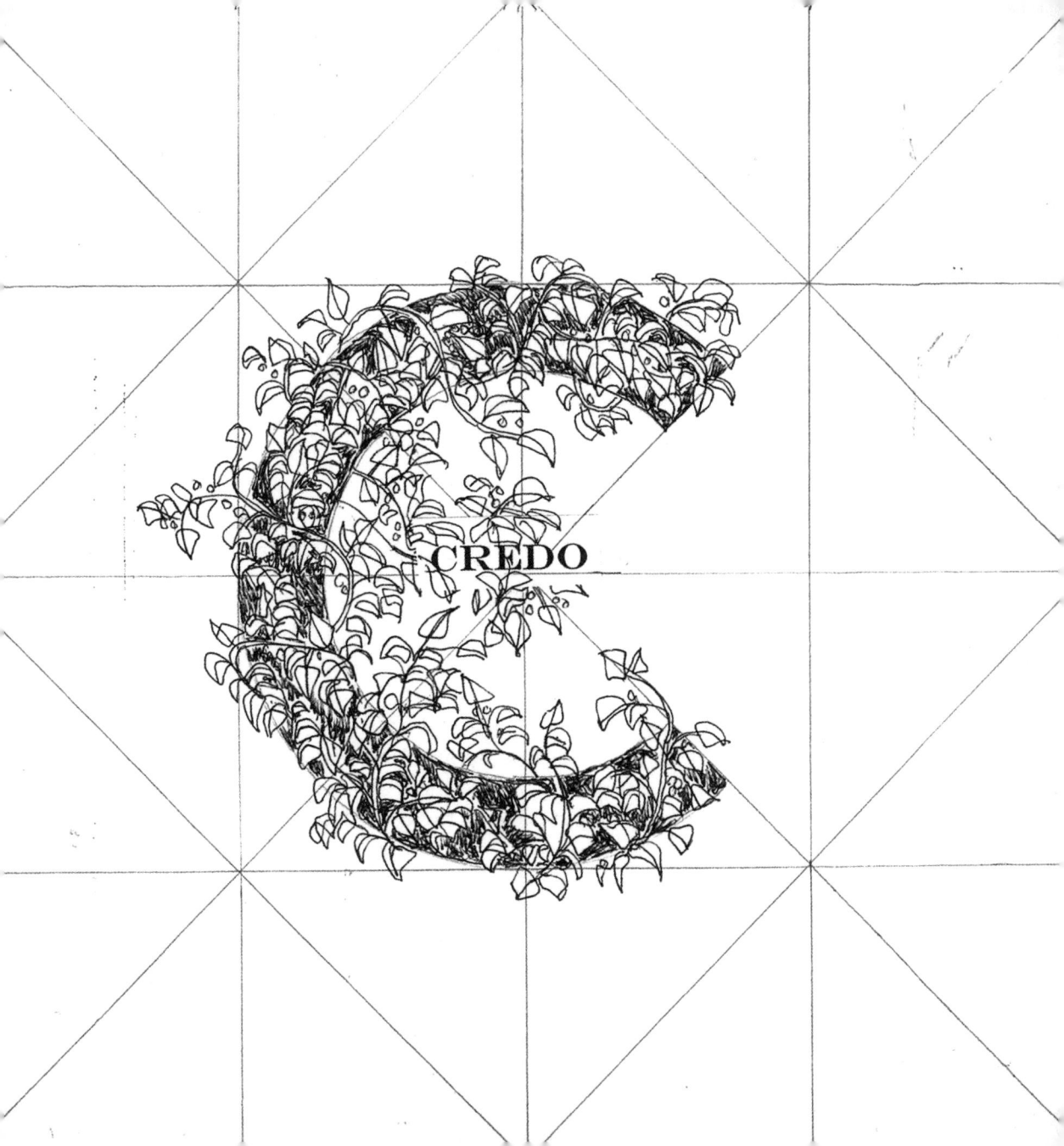

in this cleft stick

Garden of Eden
Elysian Fields
Cradle of Civilisation
Zigurattes of Urr
Hanging Gardens of Babylon
Wonders of an Ancient World
why was Jesus not born into Mesopatania
but in an arid-desert `scape of aphids
where milk & honey has long since been siphoned off

I'm demonstrating (hereabouts) with pen but not withdrawing sword

why was Abram obliged to *go west young man*
to dip into another's Med (problems there for Jonah)
to sit by wells, to sacrifice stoned son-ship

persuading her likenesses into perfect love
transforming lover from imperfect foil

opposition is not necessarily opposite
something apposite, memorable, alternative,
thoughts entwining beyond mere elasticities
barometers to declining poverties in their wonted basefulness

Abandonment
or who baptised John the Baptist

& it became as an Eighth Day &
first of spring, vernal equinox, beginning of months
on an anniversary of creation's *Bigger Banging*
softened waters oiling into Baptistries of Belief
on another stroke of dawn's Ambrosian glow
Easter's day, salvation's day, eternal day

abandon this life voluntarily & all after life abandon
luke warmness need not lead into deserts of aridity
that dangerous state where soul's propound a purgatory of errors

as Ambrose inscribes his poem onto octagonal recesses

this marks an end to all ritual washings
in its cleansing of souls central entelechy
in spirit *sans water*, dying to become reborn

prayer first & foremost for those weakening in preparation
prayer providing strength which Solomon maintained & Samson lost
with abandoning self by spinning all *things* outwith through generations

my own prayer may be only these my own poems
confirmation of my own impersonal baptism
declaration of my cleansed, my mystic spirit

John's *problematic* Word

is it always part or parcel of this human spirit
to hold at contra-distinctory times contradicting opinion
views or positions *viz a viz* God the Dog

if I'm engaged in small-talk on my way to supper
with Emmaus, these are different to those rock-cakes
Satan serves as *hors d'oeuvres* to two small fishes

but here I'm sat on his right-side, as best wine,
new bottles, opening and pouring his spirit's sense
by this, another virgin, wrapped in white with spice

once tread, there's no come-back for Mistress Gotobed

I stand by this dry creek where two waters meet
I sense a Western Stage over-mount horizon's hill
I shudder at those horses' hoofs, their snots and flecks

but now I'm seated in saloon, all warmth her smile
as smoke ascends a chimney's thick night air,
I know its safer to address these walls, their ceilings

there has never been much presence to my Lord's Prayer

it has ever been some search, my own prayer, to seek out meaning

until that Sheriff's Deputy, Apostle Paul, lowers his sad shades

Canticle of Canticles
this is not for those *Quietists*

hyperbolical, untrue, unsound
are those legion attacks upon my mystical saints

a spiritual life is not merely sanctified by scents
by flickerings of gentleness, touches of tenderness
but by grief in despondency, blindness through sadness
crimped by fellow-creatures, terrorized by temptations
experience releases a soul from disgrace into *Grace*
gravity is as God's own gracefulness to those remaining earth-bound
living their mysterious lives, receiving miraculous rewards

considering discernment of spirits with St Ignatius

soft handling matters of faith, only practice brings sufficiency
truth being Time's continuum of evening's errors of our time

perfection performs in this present past not someone's future
no other movement lies within a pilgrim's power
no control over time's ticks on God's clock-face
all progress is only passporting into humility
as stiffness of natural egotism may soften

my lord's women wove his garment without seaming
quieting all those (allegedly) fake mystic spirits

as to problematic texts

there are so many of these caught in this thicket
considering that suicide of Judas
whether he was descending from those Sons of God
unwashed in rivers of living waters
whereas this lord was supposed to draw all of mankind
towards his total abolition of wars & strifes

these are problems restive only within words
some phrase *unto this day* is easily explained away
chronicles as only somesuch decorated chronology

obviating whatever may appear to be unpardonable

as I was assured my self-same appeared as unresolved
draining from labyrinthian rocks split to spirit's blessing
as clouds pass over as fleshly lusts may ovulate

in mis-handling of money-lenders is to beckon misanthropy
handing out sops is surest sign towards excess
privilege is a liberation only for those privileged

none of this is for any impersonal interpretation
prophesy reveals implicit faith
it is our right and duty to privatize unearthly convictions

reflecting Apocryphal Gospels

& I became enveloped within a luminous cloud
as aeons of angels ministered through me
& I saw that very first luminary ruling over myriads
of those incorruptible throughout every firmament

& I was granted some temporary authority
but those virgin spirits disturb each generation
& I only had this grant of spirit for but a season
as chaos erupted to envelope their underworld

as these six stars wander around their five warriers

you see through your cloud to your starlight to lead you

there remains a nest of sparrows in my laurel tree

& that special aroma of paradise overcame me
before all *things* were to be dissolved into primeavel elements

escape your body's material confines into eternal restfulness
because where your mind rests their lies pleasures of peace

there is no point in preaching to those who remain asleep
there is nothing to be gained guarding empty sepulcres

it's time to roll away these stones of doubt

it's time to reveal this golden boy, his startled smile

de-attribution

mixed between dignified or too absurd
stretched through statis by speed
mixing paints on my new pallet
facing my own self-portrait
whiskery flakery not yet attribute
to my own hand to preserve mystique

am I a last drone in some hive despoiled
of milk of honey withholding sand with Dead Sea salts
chariots of despots destroying

or am I only some convential symbol artistically arranged

I could make my own back four to strike away
celebrities and other brats of no-sense
publishing verse in anonymity
my face-less face-book my own enigmas
as Mary packaged *Frankenstein* as her own
as Percy stole her *Show* signing off his *Intro*

are these three points to be a last recording
some other trinity to utter fruitlessness
branch shaken, seeds blown, winds whispering

a Book of Hours
or need leading to demand for a Bible in English

transposed to my visionary setting
settling amongst joys of intimacy
kneeling in veneration, imagining
devotional sweetness, mercies in familiarity

holding onto my own, my personal treasures
reflecting through golden bindings & illuminated script
handling this young calf's skinlessness
cherishing its whole embalméd soul
appearing on gravestones, ascribing on tombs

words holding sounds beyond enunciation

in this moonbeam of time's flashing
there remain shrines as markers into peace
everyone and everywhere-else snuffing out candles
or shriving of light through messages of hope
of prayer, of willingness, of service to mercy

my love's restoring opening wreathes of ripening berries
sprung amongst thorns of yellowing dried oranges
sticklets of cinnamon slicing peeled apple cores
potting on for Christmas *Poinsettias*

too many souls

this has materialised
as I shake off
hands which touch too close

this is material
casting off all clouds of doubt
to stand in uttered nakedness

this is completely inconsequential
hearts bleeding to communities
must overfill all selfishness of thought

souls drying into desert landscapes to decry

I am in a studio with unpainted canvasses
light reflects as dust lies undisturbed

I am deaf to church bells quietly unstrung
sounds denying emptying echoes of sounds

I am to be allowed to occupy my space as if
I were of only of some importance if I would add *as if*

belief belies this passion in my soulfulness
my prayer unanswered always springs to my relief

mind may ever soar above that which below has scarred me blind from *Calvary* to *Bethany*

there lies a vacuum upon which my church is built
it seemingly has unfulfilled foundations

resurrection stretching a time line through *parousia*
as minds are opened, faith unfurls
discontinuity unveiled into continuity

inspiration becomes measureless in faith
detritus into quietus
let trumpets blow their blasts to triumph
this crypt accentuates where dusts accumulate

woe or weal my lord returns for me

arrive to arrange remains to arabesque
to spice away stale herbs of death
this cross presents to me my nature's terminus
end with this empty tomb shrouded to this end

nought maintains between material & insubstantial
man must die so that through dying may arise new man

we are not raised as individual bodies
but into his whole, his spiritual *where*

all is enabled for release with bloods of watering entering all an Easter affirmation

parables point to poignant consummations
an intimacy of table fellowships
where he
whose power may save whomsoever
from God's hammer and history's anvil

His hour of fulfillment his
as fore-runner to another final revelation
standing guard against aeonian power
there is nothing to be feared nor trembled there

springing from solicitude of faith may new belief now spring

look at that light which sacred *things* cast forth
eschew all evil rituals, their *rants 'n' raves*
reconcile each soul through love to peace
cultivate piety, morality, humility,
look inwards for your own translucence

strive upwards to Olympus of your own imagining
whether you admire hundreds of gods or merely your own few
it's your own & personal hearthrug on which you kneel to pray
for blessing into spiritual revivescence

Jesus as hamper for life
not just as Christmas parcel

I had spent these late December days, *sans specs*,
outside *Fortnum's*, by the Dilly dressed with *Santa's* claws
loose change, *Big Issue*, something for a night's –
scrape, despite that caterwauling in Berkeley Square,
those clubs, their tights, crescendoes of bottle-bankings
from *Bentleys* drowned by swallowed oyster street
into *St James' Church*, whose curate melds his cure

Now I'm down bestride *St Bride's*, drowning Lutyen's cocktail shaker
up to *St Paul's* intent upon sweet Saviour's baby birth

for Abram pitched his tent before he built an altar

Reacting against not only unnecessary death & violence
but this Capital's overall profligacy in this general mess of *things*

I am at one with protest & its awkward tradition
I remain isolate on my roadway away from perdition

such cheapening of life into inherencies of war
times itself as wasteful with invisible foes of peace

But now I've peered outside my hollowed self
his hallowed face humane, divinely radiant
beams one of many inter-faithed, sublime & universal

SANCTUS

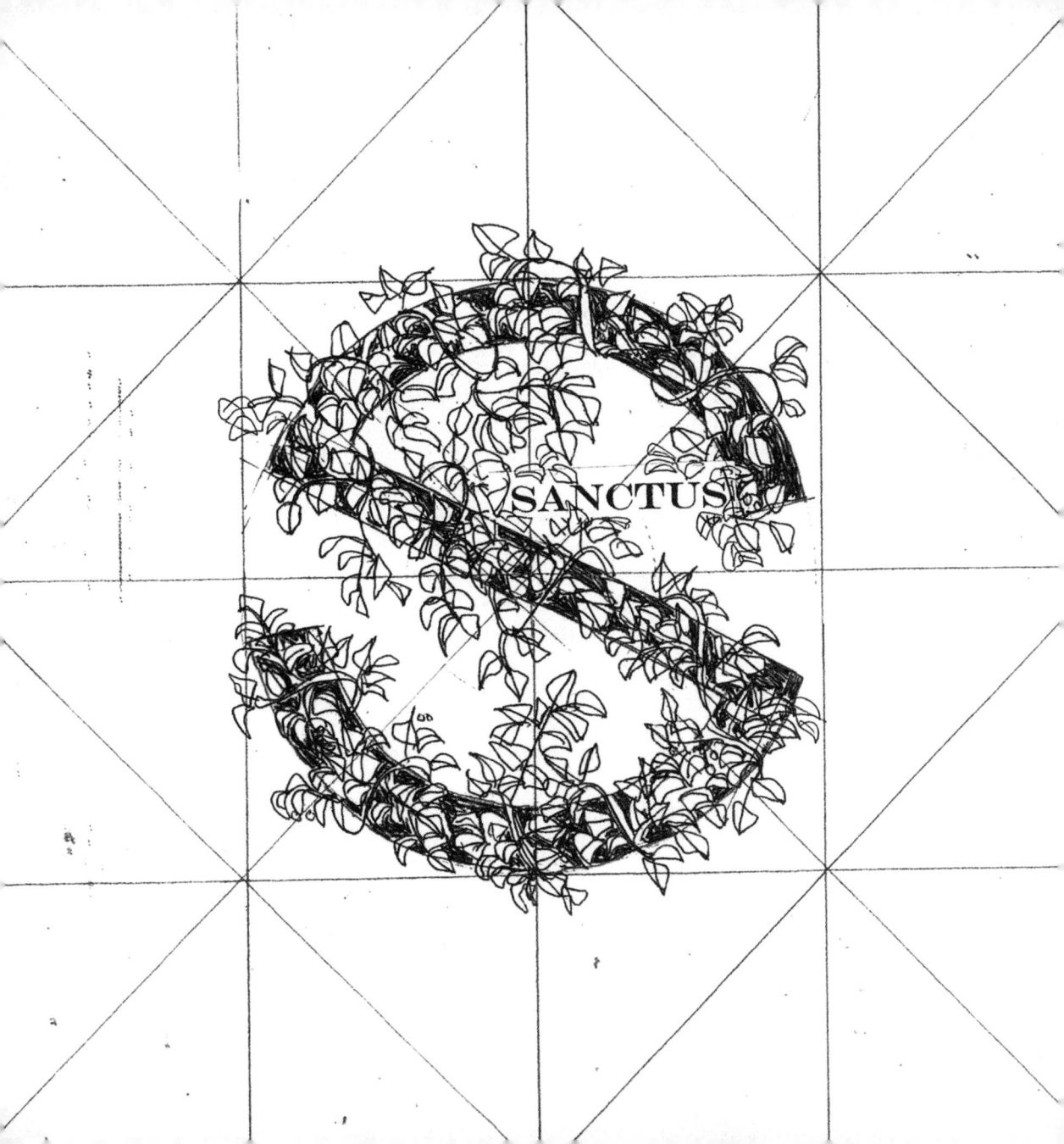

absence of Karma in Capricorn

out of reality springs some visionary soul's
feet firmly grounded to view mountainside's
mysteries to comprehend Nature's alluring sacrifices
indwelling light accentuates a pilgrim's pathways

through flowers of lifeness

always every effort each fresh effect
periodically arresting
base material, no spiritual initiate
make your night as part and parcel of your daytimes

do birthsigns have relevance save for expectancy

there is anticipation in unnatural silence
which refreshes mystic silent awe
as snowflakes fail their individual cool to meld

soft voices propel more power than emptied noise
reading not outwith lines but within words
deciphering sense from supposedly devout enhancement

how should any future be any better than this newness
whyness of heeding to understand an incomprehensible
exordium darkness expectant into unity of lightness

imaginal
my tribute (some redact) to Kathleen Raine
& her Selected Poems, Golgonooza Press, 1988

are you as timeless as your acacia tree
round which time ran so swift away

to me your gift to life is never idleness
to me within your writing of your words I'm me

as you torch your kindling fire to this world's ash
who else would gaze upon this bright belovèd face

as on a deserted shore I am ingrained with doubt
(does weight of thought always desire uneven distribution)
death most assuredly ends nothing excepting death

it's never past (tradition) it's ever new

so must I focus on imagined paradise
as perhaps it always was (and is) on Lindisfarne
seas thrashing annoyance to its chill east wind
birds piercing holy Cuthbert's soft-winged prayers

& so I seek my longed for unremembered place
(but pause in rating calculation over encaverned gods)

I love because your verse I love
your moon upborn above my sanctuary

may you now & forever remain your own & blossoming rowan tree

anima mundi

Purusha
for *Purnima*

beware each drained to mystic heart
take care of divine breathing's inspiration
that which is noetic providing knowledge
of inner ways of understanding central beings
with mantra,maxims,mottoes,
as special key words from my room of doom

reverencing lives in loves experiencing bliss
sprinkling stardust of wonderland's *rara avis*
swinging ecstatic songs into enlightenment's

unsettling and non-centering prayer

in whosoever's traditions I mix my bowl of rice
tend my *kleftiko*, annoint my brother's fatted calf
I am blessed with these pleasures of devotion
falling about me as dust in a desert of dreaming's
wonderment beneath a waterfall of mercies
with blessings, providing for unnecessary wants
my hopeless needs, my ever unfulfilled desirings
my abjectness in an absolution of resolution

my mistake has always been to underestimate mistakes

Refreshments from Rumi

I have moved from prayer to meditation
and now prepare myself for conversation
within and of and to myself as if
I were some old blanched whale trashing away seas of stress

I have released outwith my own commanding sense
everything of which those others sought to make condense

I have arrived safely into unifying spirituality
where folded blankets scent departed saints
which articulates all artificialities of being *live*

I have this prayer on my lip which only death can breathe

I have overseen my washing and my shrouding
from some earlier out of bodily experience
watching my feathered lips being undisturbed
all mirrors clothed, all bowls of water drained
sensing my candle flickering as my soul flits uncontrolled

I have overcome my foetal fear of death
and now prepare my end days with a hymn
of praise, a psalm of rest, as if
I'd wandered into some fold, secure, unshriven and at peace

His *incarnational prescence*
for *David Impastato*

your holy *en-flesh-ment* is your's wholly

finding real indirection on my pathway, foundling
off thoughts, such baggage as Jesu's name forbears,
blind camels sucking through desert sand-storms,
pausing Bedouin unwrapping their silk-lined tentacles,
uncovering some fossil-shells, enwrapped with music of centuries
watching throughout wakes of *Desert Fathers'* absent-mindedness

mine is not for making converts conscripted from deserters
mine is for revelatianory experience, for energy with exhuberance

questing this cup of Quince far into Eden's Garden

from your skies passing passages of viscerally doubts & clouds
may I unwrap your mystery in my own perplexity
in this cycle of this world's wheel as I'm unsaddled

these beget my own, my spiritual struggles
with deamons of dubiousness, paragams to persuasiveness
an ochre subscribed on bed-posts over soiled sheets

there was an absence of skittishness by their foot of his cross
toying with that puzzle through whom all must pass

Jesus retains his own lamp-post on mine own my darkling plain

veriditas
for *St Hildegard of Bingem*
as it is always sunrise, somewhere

how many more possessions do I need possess
from making mirrors for my blind towns-folk
who fail appreciation of my delicate position

these flowers for her hair provide me everything as butterfly
and so, I shall not harden my heart against aphids & fleas
as this becomes my garden of blessings, my holiness to blossomings

wandering through this wheat-field, I bend beneath their sheaves
I trill those songs which small birds strangulate
as, in my own thoughts, my sun is always shining beyond clouds

kairos not chronos

may I now breathe words which sprinkle dew-drops of promise
may my eyes open as only opened eyes may
my life be my piano on which I play white keys of truth

as I tread through grass, I feel it springing back to energise
continuing this sacredness my ancestors foresaw better than I
as my creativity is dimmed so is my bright from light

how I spend today may be how I spend my days

on a rainy Sunday afternoon, reprise dreams of immortality

life is my own & holy gift for living

theism?

in this one only sub-species of theism
where church should speak people not place
where prayer carries no shackles
where there is no bowing-down, only uplifting
of spirit in this pause after creation's big-bang

in this comfort may I wear my cassock's hood in faith
which pulled all about me teaches of its stripping-off
which lit up with joy my fear of death illuminates
as my explanation of these mysteries of life evaporates

are there too many sub-species within theism

in any emptiness there needs unifying spirituality
where none prevail over many other's pre-requisites
where Mayan astronauts Atlantis Tao refuse to fuse
where disputation is replaced by prayerful dialogue
of equals in this space bestride resurrectionalists' delights

in Krishna Mabon Christos
which of Horos Hercules & each & every other Hero
where stand they now as I approach his Judgment Seat
in my new gown of ecological awareness

Dweller on the Threshold
for *Alice A. Bailey*

of all there is and may have ever been
encapsulating your whole, your perfect personality
standing before this Gate fronting Angels of Presence
full-faced and open-eyed remaining only for a time
a season, as desires burst energies into forcefulness

everyone requires withdrawing into rest
to hold, to refuge, to processing involution
for an inner soul to proclaim its silent, its spiritual speach
to warm heart's throne for rests, for lovingness

cross into a new kingdom, enjoy qualities of kingshipness

inhabiting any place this Dweller else uninvited leaves
many fumbling fearful of dangers lurking within
be bold, Hell's darkness teems only part remembered *things*
throw out your hand, allow your spirit to expand

this door beyond this threshold always ever opening
revealing beds of spitting coals of burning frailties
run fast across, illuminate your path
wake up to greet this greater truth

of who you are and always were true you

in partibus infedelium

anyone who craves god needs to nose out some other's one
in these lands of infidels all hands are tied

tasting apples from goddess of Braji's wife, goddess of verse
assuages all loss, craftily fashioning immortality,
denying decrepitude of decay
spirit of Khids
of Moses as an Egyptian
baskets of unfruitfulness reddens parting needs
turning his key to his Pentateuch mosaic

cups of truth breaking to pieces on lips of lies

spirituality is not only province of these poor or needy
if one soul is diluted it loses none of its essential shine
as money absent of gold is alchemy
cash is that coin which entrances theatres of nihilism
from whence there can be no concealment
no capacity for universal empathy

to find an end to *things* not found
to refute god is to embrace your own devil
to be not *to have to be*

only is *God* is only

I turn to his bell-tower
its tolling echoes my toiling
I dust his mirror in my dark
its divinity distorts my mortality
I doubt I will ever feel clearly
its image being my own lack of knowing

I am conscious of this man-trap
its jaw grinning at my stumbling steps
I have entered into his sacred space

its reality, its Holy Knowledge, fills me its reality

As I walk in my lord's garden
my work shows my soul's inner-self
my words are as sighs from a sprite

As I rest in my shade in my evening
all I've learnt I must learn to forget
all I have are my memories of life's passing

As I pray in my heart for his peacefulness
he beckons me nearer his haven
he opens his arms to my worth with all of his wealth

BENEDICTUS

espadrilles
or *towards an ending of things*

for me in which form will her message be
short story, novella, something brief
or an attack of wind, wild rushes billowing
perhaps only another tear brushing her cheek bones
high & haughtiness, eyes shaded with dark sepia
stained with misuse, forbearance, regret

almost as renunciation of old or worn down slippers
before ropes fray through & anchor's away
as amongst ancient ruins sacred rituals may be rehearsed

as it becomes easier to hurry onwards into her future

I tried to twist myself through nineteen-sixty
& twist again in sixty-one
but there was ever only space for sighs
below her sleeping boards

May became June & hurrying through July to August's lateness
soon stumps *esprit de l'escalier* will be willowing

adding to this ending
in older age it is not unusual to fall
in love again within an unrequited pall

towards those *Domes of Omdurman*

I sensed I was present in some presence
is it a gift of life or love's life
which needs nothing of any intermediary

meeting with strangers is to confer ignorance
on this final fifty miles to everyone's personal Mecca
to fulfil each unfulfilled vow

by this ending of days, finding four companions
destroying idols which despoil your route
today's focus must be concentrate upon finishing *things*

silent in an inner courtyard, circle all outside

I may die here, afterwards of my pilgrimage
not to return to humdrum or mundane
but what could they, being servient, serve up as *butts*

maybe it's only this unbinding of beliefs which maybe binds
creating your own *Venus* from lumps of grey-black stone
anything may be worshipped in this ship of salts

abandon saffron robes of monastic leadership
sit inside your chosen cloister with believers' prayers
resting in this unreality of death, resisting re-incarnation

wishin' nor' nor' west

I am within my state of perfect peace
my soul as rounding to my mind's
endeavouring to be cleverer than she

These coloured evening clouds
have banked across closed skies
whatever interference from her moon, their stars
hang pendulous withholding rains

This has been too dry for summer
artificial waterings are only ever sprinklerings

one piece of brighter shroud shows through a settling sun

I draw in these combined heroic faces, attitudes
which held a bridge, which formulated thoughts

This garden holds each mystery of nature's bliss
a collared dove, a blackbird overweight
her brood destroyed, she, desolate, traduced
(how can I ever place such templates by my mind)

My ruby cat appears, her fur is agitate
all birds have disappeared
she jumps, she spits, my hound's eye's unimpressed

Seventh Seal
is this an end to me

amongst this singing & sounding off of voices swelling
oceans thundering as dazzling whiteliners ripple
suddenly his white horse his flaming eyes
redness in his sunset treading out Almighty's vines

as vinegar flesh off their riders' naked stripes
flogged into lakes of sulphur, of fires of shame
by mouth's keen knife & sceptre's sharp iron edge

symphony speaks through symbols
thorns, nails, spears, scourgings

prayers of saints bringing their feast day nearer

seven angelic trumpeters blowing their golden censer
aiding smoke from incense from presence in fire
eagles of disaster with plagues of locusts and of scorpions

through this rent veil in blindness all is revealed
alone I am in what I undertake alone
I do not search for bones, my scratchings are my relics

there must always remain this hope for some new heaven
pure earth with neither sea nor wasting shore
replacing groaning & sighing & moaning & all & every *such-ness*

Viaticum
turning another cheek

as I was praying into my own silence, kneeling
I was drowned out by his greater stillness, rising
these stones, this rood screen, all of stained glass, singing
and I am at this lynch-gate whilst twilight fading, waiting

as I am visible I may become invisible
to alter my humane for his divine
as my eyes darken, his vision brightens

I watched those whose soil despoils all decency
who desecrate only to attempt to disseminate

admit to no ancestral shrines or marbled tombs

when I came forth as Lazarus, I knew my doom,
sisters occupy their room, by Bethany
all boon deprived, each service sanctified

allowing Mary continuance, resolving human selfishness
& why of this compulsion, turning grind-stones into bread

I hear a meuzzin's cry, with pagan distant drums,
as church bells toll as weary milk-soused cows
rattle to their byre but not my bier, unrattled

my dog's breath is rank rodomontade

Isms (rarely are)

throughout this stressful storm of nights alone
wintering my soul with outpourings of dis-harmony
outposts of ghosts belying frontiers of free-thinkers
where can I piece together his presence in my own tent

I am reduced to counting donkeys on sands of doubts
as children draw sea-water to their castle's crumbling towers

behind me dunes of disbelief, their wind-swept grass be-reft
as gulls scream overhead their warnings of tsunami
of armies of re-forming angels to crucify their beast

storm & stress

I am every craftsman guilding my skills freely
I am that Ambassador from that *Faire Countrie*
which treasure-ships return to port their squalls
as merchants light up candles in their counting squares
and my wicker-chair rocks empty to a sea-borne breeze

as I lie within this coarse grass
I feel those dead breathing their last leaves
as if some spirit of this place of grief
stalks at my thought & incommodes my sense

ficciones

here is this landscape peopled with peaceful villages
villagers content or happy with their endless lot
where I am today is where I may not be tomorrow

I take my bar-stool in this inelegant *Green Man*
I share my pew in *St Saviour's* with those tone deaf
I occupy my reserved plot in my family's deepest vault

if I were to re-locate myself, an unmarked cross,
to tick away this guilt of centuries by a tree-less churchyard
if I were to be re-born, every day would be redeemed

my very own Aeolian Harp with Hopkins' sprung rhythm of breath

now here, trembling by mountain's peak
I'm surround of air, of breeze, light-headed-ness
I'm tempest, turmoil, turbulence' intensity
I'm cloud & sky, birdsong & shades of nightingales
I'm acrostic puzzle, belabouring brightness of dawn's day
I'm alone with my own self-formed conception of mortality

as each point of my compass needles me awake

I have read myself into an unholy blindness of secularities

trying to avoid being *moderne*, am I become that maudlin being where is the fate of *orality*

how can *things* emerge through sensibilities
straining this hermit in his cell
there is a hail & farewell to all green logistics
all *things* must change
albeit there is little of poetry in development

some minstrell's harp, some notes of gladness
sadness chased through wastes of silences
as pop songs lilt their wails
is there any purpose in balladry

tout court

orality has breathed her last breath
her breasts no more heaving
waisting for tunes from their dizziest movement
winds puffing sails to an idyllic mystic

cite everything, conserve nothing
search for something, not everything
finding is fun in this universal library
facts avoiding factoids

orality is *kaput*

perhaps some ultimate meaninglessness of *things*

is god only to those living not for those tone dead
finished by their sinning and buried unattoned
burnt into some devilish crematory fire

my lord embodies resurrection as living proof
through which he gives his gift of time
for my misuse through his triune God

as I bow into massed opinions
as I involve *fair play* into my concepts
as I leave all barriers safe & sound unbreached

are these becoming principles of theologies

animals experience their enormity of pain
whilst we, excessive sorrow
in unstableness of unknowingness

their constant search for food
& our inconstant assays towards those silver-tongued
maybe behind a mooncalf's smirk, her half-bleeding, half-smote side
unbalancing from here her anthropophic balances
she who may question who is he

it's not your fault (if I may apologise) this fault's entirely mine

vain repetition

in his absence, pretending *things* no longer matter
(well, for this time being, perhaps)
remain as stable as posterity determines
with each and every splash of water to my face
awakening me for blowing out of candle's snuff

I glanced him as he stole quietly outside my kitchen
pre-occupied with *pots 'n' pans*
I occupy a world too self-contained
of washing up, of scouring, Martha would be proud

therein persists my favourite of poetic trope

I'm one with Chesterton & his mahogany chest
fondling to remove her night-dress of desirability

love cools me when I'm least unready
love warms me when my frame appears unsteady

I've moved with his *incarnational presence* into his space
placed my fingers into his transcendental form
where every doctrine will dissolve in breathes of myth

when I'm retired from reciting verse
my *mañana* is that there remains some poetry of song

Inchabod
of glory once departed

several waiting in attendance bearing gifts
forming an irregular procession
as visitors arrive with curtains drawn & veils displaced
breezes drifting perfumes from uneven sands
as camels burdened for burnt journeys
hoof in impatient expectation
as tents are cushioned to a night's coolness

illuminate your life with your own candle of thought
do not presume your lord's love is freely found

prayers of oblations

observe every morning & each evening's devotions
freed from suspicions, superstitions & stupidities
fold away soiled unhealthiness of mysteries
there rests no rest in swearing into wrath
or lip-serving counting inside's out lost sheep

eschew temptation to nostalgia
kneel for prayer
enter through doors to your own, your sacred mission
knead your benison for bearing of fruit

dust & ashes

what is it
anguish & cold fear, grief in hunger
pain and poverty through wearisomeness of troubles
or simply wanting

what is worse
(without teeth dogs bark they cannot bite)
not knowing
demons in minds driven out by fright
circumventing each & every station on spent circumlocutions

watch' n' pray

these devils seize their opportunities every day
each turning second of all awakening moments
(especially as sleep succumbs)

sin's loves of beasts of sins
brevity aspiring continuous pleasures
temptations fade away as passions

my lord has seared his secrets to my heart
his riches sealing into joy my poverties
his forgiveness is my happiness into bliss

This Much I Know

that my life is as a coiled rope
that my days are as water in a pail
that my time is an extended scream from birth

in this necessity of making some material girth
in this desire to attract attention to worth
in this wanting to be achieving in growth

all that reflects is as mirage
all that is random becomes worthless
all that pretends is deception

I have encompassed my thoughts into monasteries of immutability

as I breathe out my life in days of time
as I uncoil my rope of being
as I drain my waters of living
as I voice out my own sounds

then am I revealed as a straight lie
then am I counted as a spilt pitcher
then am I expressed as a silent gasp

I have engorged information but lack knowledge

I have endured experience but have lost wisdom

Word

beginning not ending
talisman to faithfulness
precursor of truth
redeeming belief

Voice

echoing promises
fulfilling destiny
empowering ecstasies

Sounding

firm friendships in societies to scholarships
outranking kings at tables of ales of cydres
profiteering texts, humbling critics, enabling fools
enriching some *res publica* of letters some
thing not even Frankenstein could formulate as *thing*
members shape minds as others make up members'
databases, downloading fools' *paradisimo*
in scribbling rooms, candles relinquishing thinking

enthroned throughout eternity

AGNUS DEI

Ten Poems

as to the way we live now

triptych *on economics*

austerity in encumbered times
an end with money
easy cash remaining instantaneous corrupter

triptych *on politics*

as to on-street parking
as to confusions of coalition
as to porism

triptych *on society*

deliver not de-lever
attempting orderly disposals of disorderly libraries
having by-passed another ungrateful day

*in these poems I am
trying to confront (but never comprehend)
this tympany of theosophies, perhaps
it may ever only be collocation*

resumé (is 1875's craft still girt?)

austerity *in encumbered times*

I was never enabled *Heartbreak Hotel's* affordability
its environs were insufficiently inviting
But I was able to appreciate some cash in hand
its circulation round & healthy if no miser piled

Banks were large & inhospitable charnel-houses
where there were always queues of spent notes
But there were occasional faces recognizable
where sometimes responsibility was freed from captivity
and some sense of community was not only reliquary

making money may propel forwards to prosperity

Despite these arguments into a nowhere of democracy
there remains everywhere this slavery of poverty
Queuing up for welfare or jump-fronting queues
sensing a non-sense in this market-driven society
where economies of truth are scraps of wrappings on winds

austerity stings as jelly-fish, aurelia in bracken waters
its sour astringent piety inducing to asceticism

Aver its opposite, largesse with bonhomie

money's round to go round, not flat to pile

an end with money
for *economists erewhon*

money in this context means debts unjustly de-moneyed
as that Interpretation Act *male embraces female* merely misinforms
& whenever there is money abountifull surely they may

I became acutely conscious of a lack of cash in 1966
as England won a World Cup but lost to IMF on penalties
(such a mis-match to any post-match euphoria)

in austerity whatever is reality in debt can only rise
take that pound in your pocket (was Harold right? he hung that way)
borrowing to pay interest! What a novelty of nonesense!!

Capitalists will never comprehend how markets capitalise

I've heard of infrastructure bonds for multi-structure borrowings
which means as I go into Elsie Cohen's shop
to write myself (before I drop) my own internal cheque-out

I've initiated unlimited & long term loans
(for me they're sound for I have immortality)

first I present my simple choice as (there is no *firstly*)
debtors defaulting with bankers debonking
& secondly, goodly growth & fiendish inflation

pay those poor more because they debt themselves outwith of paying

easy cash remaining instantaneous corrupter
or de-constructing *post-moderne* budgets

there was to me an element of stylishness around Lord Lucan
sole striding Berkeley Square for Clermont's *lamb chops 'n' chips*
& definite panache towers over that Lavender Hill
Mob? & daring-do over Bridego's railway arch
which Brink's Mat tarnished with inflammatory threats

but now it's press on sofa's soft red button for Bingo, Poker
up that backside *instant-banking* (which presents no instancy at all)

which brings combustion to each mortal soul
(in hell those rich will try to sell to those too poor their piece of hell)

corporate suppositories for fat bellies' repositorie

are economic dogmas now refinancing maxims such as
what market gives market takes
what government taxes it too quickly waxes
increasing poverty multiplies prosperity

those rich swealtering whilst those poor must sweat
gifting a wealthy few with pennies from so many giftless

commodified communities of consumerism
present financial meta-physicians, rapacious faces
hoarding too much uncoined gold

as to on-street parking
or: *is there purpose to law*

that old-fashioned *Rule of Law* has withered & has died
now Rules & Regulations reign on roost & perch
down-loaded from that *House of Cards* which Pugin prettified
which fluctuate with Ministers' flexible fingertips

can there ever be any defence for legal co-ercion
or is that a return to reliance upon cults
of martyrs & of miracles wondering through relics

distrust uniforms, paraphernalia of power, authority discount
abiding within legislation of those philistine, impoverished

consider on-street parking & council's selling off to residents

law presides amongst those rich, preserves within those powerful
in buildings prized out from pennies from those poor
their heads as carved *Green Men* in stone & plaster
buried in towers & inaccessible as intersects
prescribing from its costly counter prohibitive proscriptions

law is not there to abuse as only tenants or trustees may
but these omni-oligarchic bankers – what law is theirs?
corrupting governments, disdaining democracy, simply bastardising

what is needed is a New Prospectus for a Really Rotten Bank

as to confusions of coalition

attitudes should be softening within hardening of arteries
ageism still stretching in this philistinian age
generation generating noisy geriatrics
un-questioning to what point is mere existence
expounding pointlessness of revolting existentialism

policies of pretence prevents politicizing partisans
instead this man of doubts defuses unity only to Hopkins' *instress*
darkened ships plying trade recognising only luminosity of light-shades
all should become beacons upon each one's own headland of sand-slip

creating coalition's Gregg-up Collider as its own creation

construct a new Babel but now of Peace which nothing can de-construct
culture is being sold for cash so collectors only fructify
as poets have their spiritual energy to diversify through poetry
Society needs to breathe more healthily in love through sociability

in this vacuum there is no-one watching Crow's Nest
Captain's drunk below & capstain's unleased so wheels go round-about

there subsists a preference for mediocre workings-out
to resupinate outside of authority or merit

first past a winning-post disappoints when only favourite's first as to porism

balancing between problem & theory bedevils politics' imbalance
innumerable solutions to incalculable solecisms

Bibles work by not dwelling upon biblical *things*
such as bodily pain or mental sadnesses
considering indigestible beings as some part of human food-chains
or whether *The Fall* as only one forward moment into onward movement or
Alaric's sack of Rome sole consequence of Christianity's attack

that balance which holds notes together is some song to time
(if songs can be spoken then she can be said to sing to herself)

nostalgia's pain is not only one pain on homecoming's nostalgic pain

time ticks in *Eden's Paradise* no time
that curse springs open only if eternal watches stop at that
my body dies on earthly tides, unlike those unburied dead at sea
avoiding eternal sufferings of pulling fingernails
when those *transhuman* have their wilfulness
& (yes) I have considered those carion carrying on in my midst's eye

in returning into notions of some *holy place*
where relics of saints martyred render all unearthy and unrede
may balance out that not seen but which may be perceived (maybe)

deliver not de-lever
*this poem contains opinions which are subject
to change without rhyme or reason*

I've contrived against so many *Squercums*
to say nothing of *Slow & Bideawhile's* remorselessness
(capitalism being causation of criminologists ´creptitude)
where responsibility for society's decline resides
where liability carries its own burden of borrowings
then ask: *at what point is growth pointless*

universes expand faster than astronomers' fat bellies
lighting candles in this afterglow of creation's burst
can *economics* exist in an economy of less-truthfulness

after negligent naughtiness of the Noughties

spotting one star through leaf-folding forest roof
keys to unlocking billions of universes beyond
provides private space for personal prevarication

I want none of this – money as an only measureable –
selling souls of mankind as their abstract ego goes
traduced into a generality of a wanting generation
squeezing some middle into burst busts, widening hips

self assessment must embrace assessing other's selves
avoiding questioning beliefs otherwise inexplicable

attempting orderly disposals of disorderly libraries
for *market forces*

I met an angry man, hooded in his cloak of cloth
I saw some angry more, who tore off others' clothes
I heard their screaming from that pit of mis-communication
I felt their pain but only in that sightlessness of those stone-deaf

all I can do is to try to stand to attention, to remain

is more debt a simple solution to existing debt
borrowing of itself is always an irrelevance
as governments cut, so money-makers collect
all fiscal austerity is as self-defeating defacement

inequality is unequated in these days of inequalities

I carry too much of debt, have lost my pension to fraudsters
no help from my State for this septuagenarian white male
asking my self what exactly is this *thing* calling itself money

I'm in my own state of fiscal impoverishment
borrowing at negative rates negates what needs to be borrowed

as an artist requires anonymity into artistry
this market is its own three-card trick of organised thieving

will there never be again that summer's afternoon
with your smiling, French windows, garden fresh

having by-passed another ungrateful day

following that ancient legend of Holy Rood which formed
his Holy Cross, being seeded from fruits
from Tree of Life (not that dubbed that fatal plant,
Tree of Knowledge of Good & of Evil)
centred in that Holy Grove of Eden's balm

Am I as Dinah's prayer in *Adam Bede*
hands stretched *abor* to Jones' *Anathemata*

'am ruinin' business on de-train
no thought of railway be de-railed
there be preachin' on de-internet
de'm fools recite de'm winds o'words
'am told de Gatz be now some eight-hour trash
'am readin' it tonight but only second class
'am sure 'dis much too long for Zelda's paws

I'll hype myself towards some huge hyperbole of pain

there was within poetries of passions some undeservedness
where those unfilled sought destinies into unavailability

there subsists questioning into an endlessness of no answering
which falls into spaces where passing time is less than forgiving

there remains only recordings of times spent & words wasted
of where anything *a spoken of* is as whisperings of leaves

there maintains some mixamatosis in this misinformation
wherein breaking out of warrens proves no breakthrough

where all envelopes into un-nothingness of utter hopelessness

resumé
(is 1875's craft still girt?)

is there progress or merely change
or are we restive within some need to know
education inclusive of so much uselessness
decaying Englishness into pleasantries of politeness
wining & dining alcoholic & immemborable whores
time for an evening's snifter in my country wastes
where town mouse never leaves his folly for a village inn

we remain only ever finite in this infinite
will we eventually appreciate an economy of *enough is enough*

have I chosen corn leaving only chaff

England has always persisted outwith perceptions of Englishness
being polite & decent, always punctual into eccentricity
but (alas) too often cautious, philistine with nervous indecisiveness

Keynes' *wings into futures* has seen Futures become things of a spent past
as greed drives growth then growth begets obesity
as manna which we cannot grub turns into grubs
perhaps we have all too easily trudged to an Everest no more

Roll Wagons West is plainly self-absorbent hopelessness
easing his back upon those treasures resounding in their East

Fifteen poems : *as three Quintets*

First Quintet: as to *infrequency of meetings*

armistice
re-union
this *thing* itself
some *via media*
of *everlastingness*

Second Quintet : as to *five centuries of protest*

of *this spiritual principle*
this *spiritual presence*
ultramontane
of *spiritual wisdom*
towards five hundred

Third Quintet : as to *an ending*

gratia infusa
ras el hanout
humour me
after *charisma*
in concluding : *on colour*

armistice

caught her view on a carriage with a small valise
(her maid was travelling seconds with her groom)
she'd been up to town to buy a gown
Anniversary Hunt with tomorrow's *Annual Ball*

she'd noticed me but with no glance to recognise
as one she'd watched abstracting apples from old Newton's orchard
as she swung to a swing from another's shove

I'd turned my dance allowed with two puffs on her terrace
but felt I'd sown a few words seeded in her selfishness

every dog has his day but a bitch, two afternoons

for I was re-visiting with new stripes & older war wounds
from my regiment as medical & non-combative
which crossed me no protection from another's cross-fire

following a ride out on that day after morning's horse
following tea in an afternoon on shore late Sunday's snooze

& I was returning in that self-same carriage with my own valise
retiring to their city and their war of words

in such shadowlands can real sunshine ever be supposed

lives are trickeries of truth within fogs of falsehoods

re-union

I met a scholar's scholar schooning alcoholic beverages
who trimmed his beard before treading his boards
there were touches of aquarette about his nose
resulting from sniffing around varieties of hallucinogenic substances

he had contrived a thesis on Kant's handbook upon masturbation
behind a purloined yet unfinished triptych by a youngish Paul Klee
which lacked any pretence towards re-assemblance towards conformity

if I were to be asked to remain as I were
then would I not remain not very much at all

how tiresome when a tired writer continues his tired writings

trying to entrap this whole universe into one line of verse
what's worse – vain glory or that gloss which once was vanity

it is only on second meetings when Chapter Two is opened
where incandescence of creativity may emerge
dialogue suspended as *poetry of thought* becomes dilated

does this rose retain her redness in my darkness
as my eyes close and her moon wanes

or what of that whiteness rising to her brightness of daydreams
as my eye blinks does she evaporate into tearsomeness

this *thing* itself
not of some *fabled muse*

here I am once more in my garden with its morning mists
where belief in one is more than error into many
where I face those wild ducks rising off their marshlands
is it only ever me or is there something else which maybe is

poetry may ever arouse those abrogated
and poets today are as pivotal as healers' hands

poetry needs must preserve our mystery, our sublimity
it endures as grass not concrete under my daily footsteps

let it remain primarily for playfulness

am I enjoying of this oh-so merry life, oh yes, I am

they stole away all my law books before considering laws of theft
in this my seventieth, my blindness opening onto Milton's light
giving due toleration for all travailing souls
faith is ineffective lacking fervour
silent meetings bringing inner soundings
remain as champions of freedom & of conscience

inherited as a trust for a believer's maintenance
awaiting a new & evangelical revival
through thought, through speech, through action

some *via media*

never deign to arrogate but ever mediate
as a tree's trunk branches into differing *arts 'n' parts*
all feel to be groping towards groupings of some elect

this is no protest against but a proclamation for this
which is an emphasis upon that belief which is
our sole salvation for our own soul
that holy apostolic chamber cleared from medieval debris
sanctioned by Church in Convention, by State in Parliament
(there is nothing of this reform in Ireland, Spain or Italy)

eraemuire facias

and in that particular circumstance of misfortune
as to a burial of their dead at sea
where committal is into renewed depths of corruption
wasting away to that resurrection which is to break
away all these vile into most glorious bodies
whereby all *things* become imbued beyond themselves

to return to their lord's folk in their fullness in worship
holding onto this *Book of Common Prayer*
which is *simpliciter* only prayer written to be read in common

of *everlastingness*

I had been walking through another couple of centuries
by burning flesh, carotid arteries & sundry simulacrum
when I was permitted pause for waters by this well-side
as a voice crossed over from some other side
he was that younger brother far from home
but seated, his eyelids drooped as low as night-shade

In those days there was no cause for pausing in their light
with nights too dangerous for sleep, cry of a night-hawk

I saw myself translucent as will 'o' wisp on my moor

whilst in their shadow's Cathedral candles betoken

These were their earliest texts, placed in their mother tongue
those who were not blessed, remained perplexed

I've wrapped these pages into clean pressed sheets
that folded linen lies too soft by a pillow cold as stone

Those spent years as famished pilgrims wend their way through weald
at night each light turns off to fright or blight

Is my ending a mere reflection of my beginning
am I ever able to transform myself
or is my silver's die cast dead in diamond

of *this spiritual principle*

differences are not merely of obstinacy & caprice
but are as propellers of conscience & of principle

these activities of spirit are not confined to any apostolic age
go forward as David and destroy that Goliath within

nakedness in dreaming brings forth purity in vision
personal light as doctrine of inner divinity
not those medievalists with their erotic mysticism
but evidencing indwelling spirit of word of life's fullness
cherishing all & every charismatic

Lord as Spirit

in faith, deride doctrine, cast all aside as faithlessness
drinking into this libation of immortality
believing only into belief itself

trying into kindness, this sad word spits unkindness
so my soul's base lacks permanent but restive displacement
it abides no neutral territory

nationalism can never substitute religion
governments play in miniature, my lord cherishes minutia

I promise myself my own life's work as Luther's abounds in paradox this *spiritual presence*

this Bible is not intended to be a thesis of absolutes
enticement into Doetism, that unreality of being
this Bible is its own paradox of mysteries

let this sacred intersect each & every daily step
evensong's spirituality & matin's harmony
multi-task in words & song, in poem & psalm

foster peaceful neighbours & trustworthy friends
try to emulate vindication of early evangelists & martyrs
dull iron glowing with glorious fire divine

montes pietatus

studying over this bar my chemistry of cocktails
groundswells of poety pierce through this silence
man's will being his final approbate
only works ever evidencing faith alone
men's problems are those of each and every man

enjoying daily communion
endorsing private prayer behind closed doors

free will objects & over-rides salvation

grace saves

ultramontane

searching always for tolerance beyond these mountains
baring individual thought & intellectual freedom

each island is conjoined by its continental shelf beneath
every word expressed is contained within our own subconscious

each monastery stood separate and intact and vulnerable
every sect is now its own wave on this sea of faith

in separateness, in diversity, germinates unity of purpose
living persons meeting perceive life in other persons living
dense uniformity of law denies dynamic spontaneity of creativity

nothing is solvable by flippancy or humanity's capricities

does discussion always dissolve into division
is there any hurt or harm in embracing disunity
every truthful mouthful grinds upon its teeth of doubt

there is no such thing as the history of religious thought
making nonsense of this so-called sense of being or *Wisdom of the World*
(this always confounds an elder brother supping his own & fatted calf)

I proclaim to & of this *Good News*

I do not need to protest against each Papal Bull

would that my whole life be my own reversal of *Syllabus of Errors* of *spiritual wisdom*

there is no folly but much wisdom in trying to spot cloud
to follow an Autumn's moon wandering through stars

wonder remains as fulcrum of all of passion
as in a field grown wild a lazy farmer garners
naught but envy of prosperity of others more wicked

walking in two is good medicine for both
rubbing a rubric into sores of dis-satisfaction
valuing sage & saint, prophet & poet
education has failed to promote any appreciation of wisdom

who is that persona bestride those skirts of Lady Wisdom

in fear of your own lord begins your own wisdom
accepting plurality into all aspects of tradition

each time of teaching touches flames from Pentecost
universities stand proud in churches but poor in prophesies
there is a lifetime in scholarship before sense prevails

those fond remembered phrases of he who loved to live
with those poor or handicapped or just outside

in whom by whom through whom and for whom
this world was made to be as this

towards five-hundred

when a date is expressed as when
only once can it stand as one only

there are ninety-five reasons pinned there
which frighten doubters into a burning of witches

and their cattle will trample down any new hands
lands occupied by force are never safe-house lands

prayer's called upon when there's needed more than prayer
but doubts are rarely counterpoint by re-uttering doubtful buts
is this justification for averring *what is this*

adorned this door to new dawning

might rage and hate always be resolved by might
or can mediation retrieve this boat's oar

scribes have interlined their prejudice prescribed
scholars sharpen up tongues to scholarships
do consonants kneed if vowels do

to my own frailty I prostrate myself separated into two
one before salvation but now completely one

protestants protest
that *Holy Apostolic Church* was never that

gratia infusa
for *Parson Thwackum*

deus absconditus
to me can only and ever be
deus revalatus
upon that needle's point which spins upon my heart's

faith & order – life & work
twentieth century's ecumenical mirage
oppressor's wrong or proud man's contumely
these prescribed means to grace are too often of sacraments
I am as his lost cause, ungodly, confounding all logicality

enmity across first cousins is easiest to cross out

does this evolve new handwritings before grazing of grasses
faith being ever only one personal experience
demanding of total commitment
squeezed into too many straight-jackets of feastings of fastings
with witchcraft wandering within her wardrobe
his secular with her progenitor of paganism

now to serve that body of Christ with this my mind of Man
searching through Sibylline scripts
will there be governance in that messianic Kingdom

ras el hanout

from this souk's shade, skies reflecting seas,
blueness or whiteness especially freshness of fragrance,
each day's goodness scintillates as every best spice does

nothing should be taken for granted in this way
as there may be too soon no more day
flash of a surgeon's steel cutting away herbacious borders

extracting all bodily fluids, draining away all badnesses,
where, speaking from memory, life is one long contradiction,
where clouds of doubts obscure a mid-day moon's observance

in a circled room there are no escaping corners

cupping my face into this folding of my hands
which close away from an opening of another day
considering a clock's tick in no moonlight on six bells

mirrors holding only pastness, their polish tarnished,
whilst walls of rooms contract into my client's cavities
my brain brewing up into a broth of tumultuousness

in this false calmness which subsists as my own bed-chamber
dare I now construct my own ending to this my own life's poem
sheets' careful folding belie past presence of my lord

humour me
of concinnity with a soupçon of eurhythmy

there sighs astonishment on at last arriving there
where those to tarried to abeyance are now no-where
to be overheard on this crowded quayside where no-one wants to be

there is a time to try to walk away from there
but knowing where throws up the doubter's *but*
to circumnavigate is merely to return to where I've been to

I begin to compile a list of errors & omissions which I
in these strayings into by-ways, settling in old Inns
by Settles protecting warm ales from those fires which have burnt bye

unless my greatest felony is unrequited love, naught-less

I have been within an aloneness mostly of my life, I have
been betrayed & deceived more often times than believed have been
there were always those applying mendacity to get there

mind's only loneliness is inside a lonely mind
escaping from myopia requires more than optical escapades
raison d'etre into lies & frauds belies all reason

open lips conceal cooled breathes from hearts cracked open

standing alone remains all that I appear to have done, notwithstanding

balance what remains in life's scale against death's emplied balance

after *charisma*

is this all there is

due his first birthday he was almost nearly two
his time-clock always ran too fast
& now his three-score years & ten kicks in
he's kicking buckets in his reckoning of palish undertakings

yet there never dawned for him morning of an Eighth Day
as his nights were only realised within readings
or his daylights wronged with writings
as he had failed to breathe her offered mandrake

& she on turning down his linen & cries is that it

maybe it's enough to sow this present into some pleasant land
& not presume to grant some peasant his eternal life

maybe reading for divinity is too divine conceit
& just admitting morality's only mortgagable (sub-prime) asset

sapiential studies may be heralding prophesies of love
or is this acculturation my real revelation
will my part of his heaven ever be leavened with me *Right Here on Earth*

a body must be healed before its soul be saved

& she turning off his grave & sighing ends *is that all*

in concluding : *on colour*
for my Illustrator

too much blood in that *Holy Book* too little colouring
leaving concepts of dark ironies as inconsequent as sand on glass
prayers as testaments to singing of pigments, chanting of tones

yet those *Illuminated Manuscripts* burn with purple bright with gold
but *Inquisition* focuses itself only upon that which it mustn't see
those qualities in salts as *Spanish Gold* which slake as shadows

persons passing painted canvasses throw over shade to light
drawing their own shadow of conformity while canvassing taste
parting (in their blue jean's tease) *Mercury Blue* as visions of imagination

on brickolage

one purpose of painting is to confuse others into colour-blindedness
to communicate in some strange tongue to those stone-deaf
there rests an alchemy which by dividing, unifies
it is as mixing pigments on an artist's palette as his pinxit

colour is inside myself as is taste & smell & touch
I may see some coloration which you may only imagine I may see

success of a work of art
often is inherent in its initial failure (*often is*)

so here's to rubricating all of this into my own, my chiaroscuro

Addendum

*It is not to be supposed
that two thousand men,
pick them as you will,
should be all of a mind*

Edmund Calamy's *The Grounds of Nonconformity of the Ministers who were Ejected.*

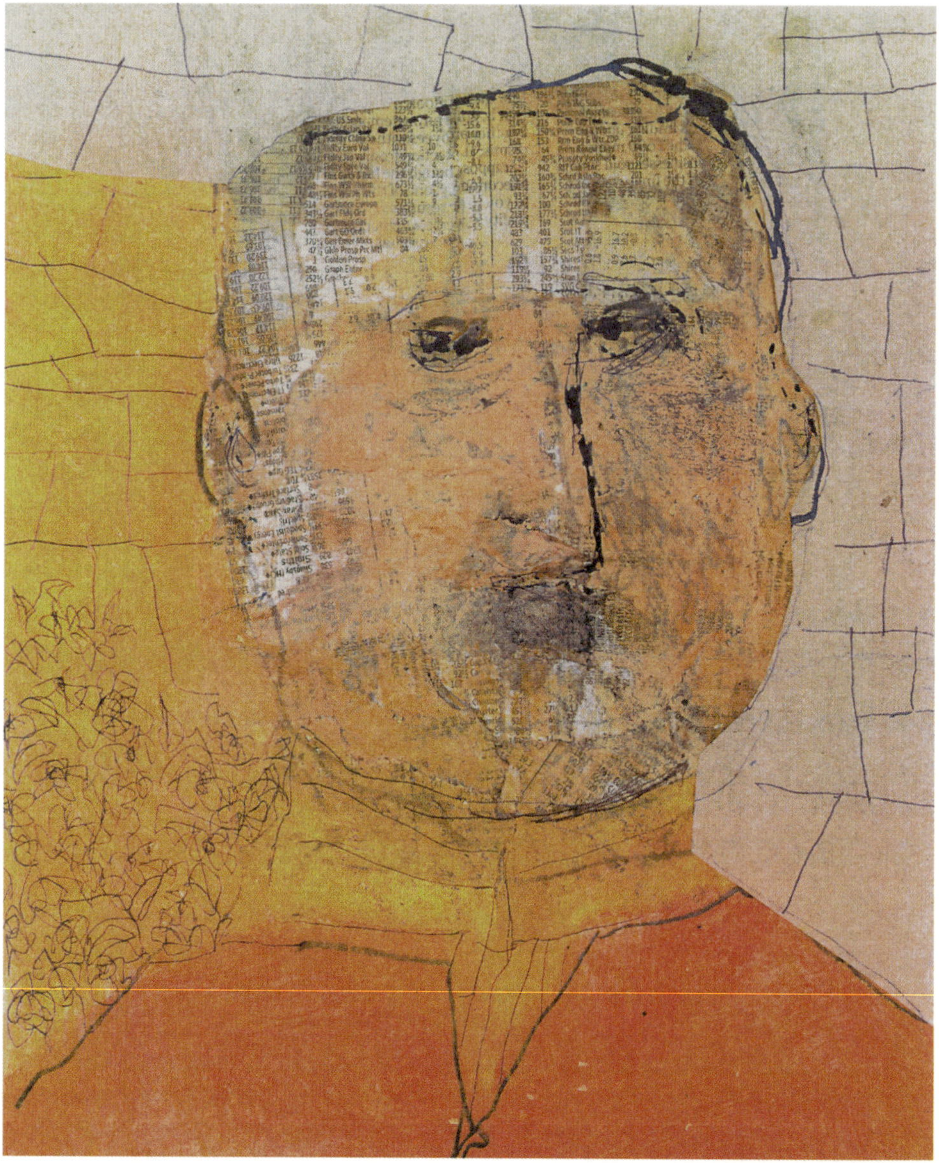

Afterword

Is divided into three parts: first, to describe how this came together, secondly, to describe its layout and, thirdly, to present what I believe it may be.

as to origins

This collection began as a submission of 22 poems to the 2010 Poetry Business Competition which is orchestrated by Poetry North and as I was born in Consett, County Durham, I supposed that their concept of *North* embraced me, but the Adjudicator was not so embraced. I posted them that year on *Diwali Day*. Incidentally, that was the first time the *Festival of Light* had fallen on *Guy Fawkes* since, I think, the early Seventies when I was living in Fulham and an engaging Indian family next door asked if I would be *doing fireworks*. Not really, but could they and there was astonishment that not only did I know of their *Festival* but, when the head of those *family members* visited and *lit up* in my library and saw the *Upanishads*, Tagore *et al*, there blossomed a close friendship until cheap cigars and *Chivas Regal* took him out, as they have done to other young Indian entrepreneurs whom I have been fortunate to know.

I've explained in the *Note* on the Illustrations how at Midsummer 2011, Winston provided me with some Images which, he explained, were inspired by lines from T.S. Eliot's *The Hollow Men*. Of that poem Stephen Spender[1] says it "is a kind of coda to *The Waste Land*" and so I applied those as a not dissimilar coda to my poems. Further pieces followed, as they will, and a dozen which I provisionally sub-titled *Mystical* came together almost as some entity and it may be not without interest that they, here, comprise *Sanctus*. In May 2012 I submitted *Mystical* to the Templar Pamphlet & Collection Awards. Previously I had sent a selection of some of the other poems to the *New Criterion* Competition in August 2011 and others I had circulated privately and read to friends.

The next step in the development of this work was my attending the opening of the *Pre-Raphaelites (Victorian Avant-Guarde)* Exhibition at Tate Britain in late 2012. It was at that time that I introduced as a sub-title my reference to *Chants*[2] after William Morris as I continue to be a life-long Fabian Socialist. I was moved by how disparate was my present experience to that at their previous showing in 1984, which I attended, but, perhaps, that is for somewhere else.

I thought I had completed *Homily* on 13 January 2013 but when I picked it up again after some eleven months I felt that its division into five, being,
  Secular, Textual, Devotional, Mystical, Capsular,
was artificial and seemed to be a barrier betwixt *poem 'n' reader*. I have therefore re-arranged these poems into six new *Units*, following Denise Levertov's *Mass for the Day of St Thomas Didymus*[3] as,
  Kyrie, Gloria, Credo, Sanctus, Benedictus, Agnus Dei,
because *Reformation* is not separable from *Mass*. Not wishing to either repeat *Preface* or Illustrator's *Note* I would explain that I have chosen the first letter of each of those words for these *Decorated Initials* which I hope provides further linkage throughout this work. How a collection of poetry is conceived and voiced remains a mystery which I have endeavoured to resolve by recording the steps in the evolution of this volume.

as to layout

I now expand upon my reference to the *Mass* which provides the sub-titles for these six *Units*. There is not much singing in the *New Testament* until in the book of *Revelations* a glimpse is given of the heavenly liturgy, where *Hosanna* is sung ceaselessly before the throne of God. I have adapted that musical module which Johann Sebastian Bach perfected in his *Mass in B Minor*. I must breathe this softly because I hear an echo of
  Mark 14 v26   *and when they had sung an hymn*
           they went out into the mount of Olives

It is the celebration of the *Last Supper* which was intended to be the symbol of the unity of the *Church* but it is the form of its performance which has become the source of disunity. Putting aside such mischief as the sale of *Indulgences* and political intrigues and other chicanery of the 16th Century, the *Reformation* emerged out of cardinal disagreements over the *Eucharist* and, sadly, those differences endure and today, alas, remain an impediment to the ecumenical movement, which I pray these poems may progress. Simply, that His *Supper* be celebrated by those two or three gathered together in His name, with Himself central, but, I must remind myself that this is to be *homily* not *sermon*.

My layout is central to my own celebration of *Reformation*, now approaching its five hundredth anniversary, and it has caused me to compile this Collection, by concentrating how through *faith* differences in *belief* may be side-lined (perhaps, even, *sent-off*, to move towards a pursuit which does have *mass-appeal*).

as to content

My working title for this Collection was *Around some 39 Articles* which became *Lachesis*, being that one of the three Greek Fates who assigns to mere mortals their fate or destiny. After I adopted *sola Scriptura* from William Tyndale's Appendix to his preface to his 1534 Revision of the New Testament[4], and reading further in Gerald Bray's book I took from that another working title *Homilies* out of Thomas Cranmer's *A Fruitful Exhortation to the Reading and Knowledge of Holy Scripture, 1547*[5].

> *The least that can be said of the Homilies is that they are of more authority than any sermons preached by particular clergymen, seeing that they are the Church's own sermons, showing how the facts and doctrines of the Word of God are to be brought home to the consciences of men. But even their statements are to be brought to the test of God's Word, seeing that ignorance of God's Word is the cause of all error. It is true that the Homilies cite the practice of the early Christian Church and the opinions of the ancient*

> Christian Fathers, but, faithful to the vital principle of the Reformation, they regard the Holy Scriptures as the supreme authority in all matters of doctrine. And in this sense it is true, however much denied, that 'the Homilies direct us to the Bible only' [6]

That quotation remains relevant to me because although I was not indoctrinated into the Church of England I was into that more schismatic of Open Brethren who base their activities (or more often lack of them, as prohibition maintains their forté) upon that translation of the *Holy Scriptures* prepared for King James (*First* of England, *Sixth* of Scotland). That was my formulation but, as I illustrate in *Nocturne*, I've moved into and through many other and beneficial texts. It does not matter where you start (we don't have much say in that) it's what you end up as which is pertinent. Shadows of thoughts left behind are seldom clarity in retrospect.

I felt that that word *Homilies* was too specific and so too restrictive because of its historical background and I have explained in the *Preface* why I have chosen this especial word *Homily*. I cannot over-stress how much of *Reformation* framed and formed my own emergence from fears of childhood into my present frailties. This is, therefore, my excuse for making this presentation: it would be presumptuous to expect that it becomes some small part of an appreciation or, to use *new-speak* to *begin to deconstruct* (whatever that is intended to convey). It is for others to *wend their way* but for me:

> *not all poems are dressed for sex*
> *some style bow-tie, even uneven cravat,*
> *others armchairs by safe-soft fire-sides,*
> *not all excite extremities.*

It is difficult to focus upon *Reformation* as a *Pilgrimage of Grace*, especially with the *Church* in England becoming a mere Department of State, situate somewhere elsewhere in those *Corridors of Power*. I need to look at its effect on *nowadays*. I don't think science helps in this: it produces ever more clever contrivances; the capacity to exchange information quickens, but the ability to apply knowledge, appears to slow.

These are issues *Poetry* should not only address but attempt towards, if not solutions, understandings: exhortations to enable moving forward, onward, upwards. Some say *live not on dreams but on convictions*. I say live through your own soul and embrace its dreams and you may well become convinced (of what, it's not for me to say).

Taking what some may consider is a somewhat arbitrary date for the *Reformation* as 1517, is it not remarkable that the foremost English dramatist (and some would add *Poet*), writing as he does at the close and turn of that Century, sets no play upon its Stage save, perhaps, for his own aside in *The Phoenix and Turtle*. Is this an historic reason (to apply a poor pun) why its present effect is being played down. Does anyone want to be reminded of its consequent wanton destruction with blood-baths of torture and execution.

I have recorded elsewhere that I view my work as being some *continuum*. The riddle is that I do not know how far I may have riddled. Stepping aside from that *wholesomeness*, I do believe that each poem should speak for itself. But there is no reason why individual poems as voices should not be gathered together into a choir and that is what a volume of poetry attains towards, a collective chorus rather than individual solos. I have spent the greater portion of my adult life (and is there any other?) in writing poetry and, for a shorter season within that span, publishing the poetry of other poets[7], and so, now, find myself deep into a dense wood where branches obfuscate. I feel that this attempt towards a gathering together, apples making cydre, bees producing honey, becomes of relevance in the message which poetry *speaks*. In its distilled form, it is silence on a sheet of paper. It is for lips to lick. There is no encumbrance in speaking these words aloud or mouthing them into an eternal *wantingness*. Nothing detracts: that volume exists; each poem maintains.

In writing of spiritual or mystical matters, although that which is material must not be neglected, avoid affectation towards interpretation. This is my belated contribution to *ascetical literature*. At the end of this and every other day, a poet may only be measured by the length of his line. I hope these amount to more than mere *Theosophy*. I have attempted to avoid *Hymnology*. As to that, I remember an old "brother" officiating (and that is the precise cord to strike) at a funeral when a requested tune (to use an all embracing word) was struck up on the *wooden brother*, to whom he declaimed *nothing false here* and another (younger and soon to be *read-out*, excommunicated to those of the Catholic but not necessarily catholic persuasion) muttered (he was not so forceful) *then, out with your false-teeth*: so much for false prophets.

It's almost four years since I signed off the *Preface* to *Feasts of Devotion*. A total of 95 poems in return for 4 years labouring in the *Vineyard* does not constitute a harvest. I suppose, milking another, it's *writalinaversaday*; but my poems do not emerge with that regularity of habit. Indeed, it is too easy for me to drop the habit of writing off my shoulders and habitualise the work of others.

Maybe, re-reading the other *Prefaces* or *Afterwords* to my previous ten collections, I have commented sufficiently on my own poems, especially the twenty-one pieces of prose I wrote to accompany the nineteen poems which comprised *bring back to the way* and which I closed on my 62nd birthday: they remain as signposts into and through my work.

Poetry remains as *the* unending dialogue, prepared prior to prayerful-response. In this mystery of faith some are enabled to hold their certainty of belief. For others, the text itself suffices even if, in their oblation, echo unanswered cries for peace, for mercy.

It is that greater beyond which poetry must attempt not only to reach but to popularise, to introduce an internet sound in which lurks sense. I do so deliberately because sounds lacking sense is only noise: I seek the songs of the soul. I ask myself: why must everything have to be so *quick*? I am part of the eternal dead, not of the tick of time. Within *Poetry* is the turning of the seasons; there is no room for the artificiality of a calendar year. May I represent this pictorially: those with faith rest safely in their beds; those seeking belief are outside on the streets shooting unbelievers.

What I've centred upon in my own writing, is a form of my own continuous *Reformation* because what I write today grows out of what has seeded in my mind's yesterdays. Now that my collection is complete, I've revisited *The Hollow Men* and have chosen two of Winston's *Images*: for the front looking to the future; at the rear, regarding some past.

I close with a word upon *Agnus Dei* where I'm endeavouring to focus, *après* Trollope *as to the way we live now* and in the final three *Quintets* are my personal thoughts on the society which, alas, I have helped to create. There is a shadow of sadness in these my last poems. Is that because there is no forewarning of *Reformation* in Scripture?

This is not to attempt to challenge creativity which has its own especial stimulus; the purpose of this *Afterword* is for the walker or hiker, resting in the *Snug*, to assimilate, which is the only purpose for the continuing existence of a *Wayside Inn*. To conclude, these poems attempt a pilgrimage from ideation, through texts and by spiritual to find some mystical. All is as a personal search towards some form of *Sanctuary*, not unlike seeking the wisdom of the *Seat Perilous*…

Snowdon Barnett, The Pavilion, Kintbury, 28 February 2014

1 *Eliot* in *Fontana Modern Masters,* William Collins Glasgow, 1975.
2 *Chants for Socialists*, Socialist League Office, London, 1885.
3 From Jay Hopler & Kimberley Johnson's *Before the Door of God, An Anthology of Devotional Poetry,* Yale University Press, USA, 2013.
4 Gerald Bray *Translating The Bible,* Latimer Trust, 2010 p.7
5 ibid p.92
6 From the *Witness of the Homilies* (Church Historical Society) as quoted in *The Protestant Dictionary*, Harrison Trust, London 1904.
7 *Rivelin Retrospective*, Rivelin Grapheme Press, Kintbury, 2012.

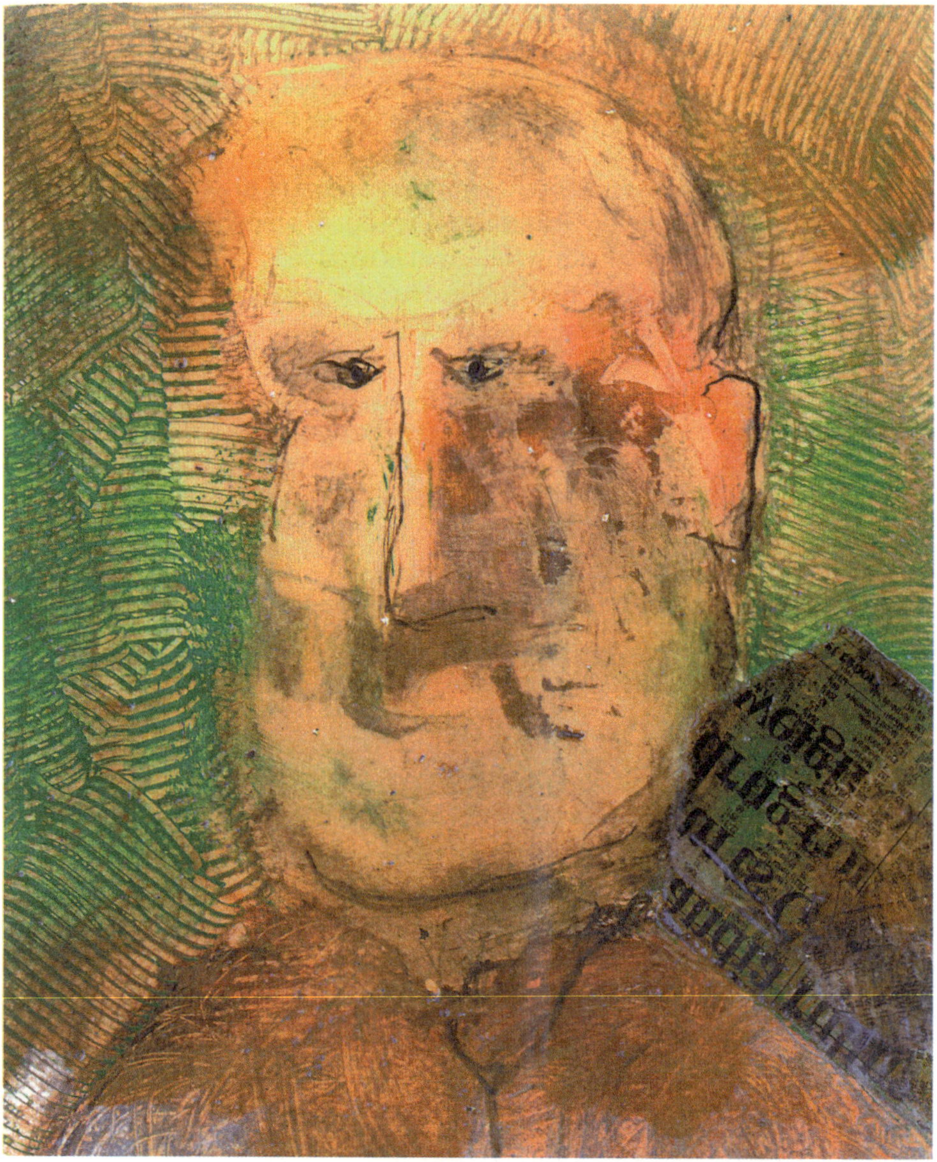

The Author's published poetry

Lines on the Colour Turquoise
(autobiographical lyric)
Last Entry
(Romance of Antarctica and Captain R F Scott)
Lapis Lazuli
(vexato quaestio)
Dossiers Secrets
(gnostic tract in verse)
with *The Argument*, published simultaneously
Hiroshima Hypostasis
(a poem for the Millennium)
Poetry Chapbook
(choice from forty years of writing verse)
Once in a Blue Moon
(BiMillennium Poem)
Now is as it pitches
(reflective lyric)
Nocturne
(devotional and prayer-poems)
Feasts of Devotion
(aid to worship)

with *(as Editor)*
Rivelin Retrospective
(Chronicle & Bibliography of the Press)

Snowdon's work can be obtained from Rivelin Grapheme Press
jsb@snowdonbarnett.com

post tenebras lux